RE/MARKS ON POWER

RE/MARKS ON POWER

HOW ANNOTATION INSCRIBES HISTORY,
LITERACY, AND JUSTICE

REMI KALIR

THE MIT PRESS   CAMBRIDGE, MASSACHUSETTS
LONDON, ENGLAND

The MIT Press
Massachusetts Institute of Technology
77 Massachusetts Avenue, Cambridge, MA 02139
mitpress.mit.edu

© 2025 Massachusetts Institute of Technology

This work is subject to a Creative Commons CC-BY-NC-ND license.

This license applies only to the work in full and not to any components included with permission. Subject to such license, all rights are reserved. No part of this book may be used to train artificial intelligence systems without permission in writing from the MIT Press.

The MIT Press would like to thank the anonymous peer reviewers who provided comments on drafts of this book. The generous work of academic experts is essential for establishing the authority and quality of our publications. We acknowledge with gratitude the contributions of these otherwise uncredited readers.

This book was set in Stone Serif and Stone Sans by Westchester Publishing Services. Printed and bound in the United States of America.

Library of Congress Cataloging-in-Publication Data is available.

ISBN: 978-0-262-55103-8

10 9 8 7 6 5 4 3 2 1

EU product safety and compliance information contact is: mitp-eu-gpsr@mit.edu

For Ebony and Ade
In Memory of Ryan

CONTENTS

ACKNOWLEDGMENTS   ix

1   OPENING REMARKS   1

2   HER MARK   23

3   MARKING BOUNDARIES   45

4   MARKED MEN   71

5   BOOK MARKS   95

6   MA(R)KING NARRATIVES   119

NOTES   145

INDEX   171

ACKNOWLEDGMENTS

I am the beneficiary of generous care and wisdom bestowed by cherished colleagues, friends, and family. My many joys writing this book reflect that truth.

When I was a wayward teen, Jeff Kupperman, Fred Goodman, Jeff Stanzler, and Michael Fahy welcomed me into my first academic community, the University of Michigan's Interactive Communications & Simulations group. You recognized my need to ask new questions and play different games. My growth as a student, then teacher, and eventually as a scholar remains rooted by your collective mentorship. And Jeff—by contributing to your dissertation research twenty-five years ago, I first experienced writing as conversation, as a social endeavor. You welcomed feedback from a high schooler and immeasurably altered my confidence as a learner. Your commentary on an early version of this manuscript typifies your enduring and valuable counsel.

This book extends conversations that transpired between 2016 and 2021 as part of the Marginal Syllabus. Thank you Christina Cantrill, Cherise McBride, Michelle King, and Joe Dillon for deepening my understanding of annotation, literacy, and learning. Our project succeeded because of your vision and leadership. I'm also thankful for support we received from the National Writing Project, the National Council of Teachers of English, Hypothesis, and the authors who trusted us to read, annotate, and discuss their scholarship. I'd be honored if previous Marginal Syllabus participants turned their attention to this open-access text; please, annotate it.

I'm still baffled when recalling how Antero Garcia pitched me on pitching a book to the MIT Press. We bounced that idea around at the 2018 AERA Annual Meeting in New York City, and then wrote what became our book *Annotation*. Thank you, Antero, for introducing me to this amazing press, collaborating on many projects, and for adding that sticky note to my office door.

May we all be so fortunate as to learn alongside scholars like Manuel Espinoza. Profe, when you read this work and told me I was writing "the longue durée of annotation as a primary human activity," I smiled with gratitude. Why? Because the gift of your good word, so incisive and frequent over the years, is a true blessing. Faith plus action will propel our steps forward.

In the fall of 2016, Francisco Perez walked into my office to discuss research. In the spring of 2023, we walked into Tijuana through the San Ysidro Port of Entry. It's implausible tracing how we got from one place to the other, just as it's impossible predicting where we'll share our next meal. Francisco, you're a real mensch. I couldn't have done this without you.

Jeremy Dean and Nate Angell were instrumental stewarding my entrance into the worlds of social annotation and open education. You both thoughtfully organized my stint as Scholar in Residence at Hypothesis during the 2020–21 academic year, and you've vouched for me on too many occasions. Yes, Jeremy, it was your question that inspired me to craft the core arguments of this book. And Nate, I hope my words do justice to your uncompromising moral clarity.

Dear friends and colleagues have obliged my obsession with annotation and, lucky for me, replied with their good sense. My thanks to Chris Andrews, Kira Baker-Doyle, Maha Bali, Robin Brandehoff, Ben Devane, Justin Hodgson, Ty Hollett, Betina Hsieh, Alan Levine, Charles Logan, Chris Rogers, Tim Saunders, Dane Stickney, and Mia Zamora.

I'm indebted to many other individuals who guided the writing that appears here. Kate Clifford Larson offered grace and encouragement in response to my chapter about Harriet Tubman. My thanks as well to park rangers at the Harriet Tubman Underground Railroad State Park and Visitor Center. Research for my third chapter was assisted by Carissa Pastuch,

Reference Librarian with the Geography and Map Division of the Library of Congress, and also by Carlos Alberto Flores Martinez and Juan Antonio Hernandez Ambriz of Archivo Histórico de Tijuana. Chapter 4 came together because of Ashley Daniels-Hall at 826 New Orleans. Alaina Lavoie, with We Need Diverse Books, edited two #SharpieActivism blog posts that established a foundation for my fifth chapter. That chapter was initially developed for the volume *Literacies in the Platform Society: Histories, Pedagogies, Possibilities,* edited by Phil Nichols and Antero Garcia. And Shea Swauger affirmed that my foray into critical librarianship was accurate and useful. Dorothy Garrison-Wade, Associate Dean at the University of Colorado Denver, directed my path through tenure and toward sabbatical with distinctive mentorship.

I drafted this manuscript while on sabbatical in Cambridge, Massachusetts, throughout the 2022–23 academic year. To the staff at Cambridge Preschool of the Arts—and beloved Morahs Elkie, Ashley, Christine, Emma, and Eliane—we sincerely appreciate how you cared for our young toddler with unwavering kindness and endless art projects. Jess and Andrew, Jenna and Ron, and Meena and Ndubueze remain the very best of friends. Mr. Ray at Christina's kept our family nourished with the spices of life. And Justin Cerenzia and Devon Ducharme graciously invited me to visit Rhode Island, again and again; early mornings at Sachuest Point cleared my head and provided much-needed solitude.

This book would be incomplete without contributions from many people who agreed to an interview, answered my email, confirmed details, or permitted my use of an image, including: Carolyn Bailey, Hakim Bishara, Alexandra Bowditch, Sarah Bukrey, Lynda Claassen, Alex Criqui, Amy Dickerson, Quinn Dombrowski, Alex Gino, Megan Honey, Christopher Hunt, Sarah Leavitt, Courtney McClellan, Laurence McGilvery, Mark Priest, Debbie Reese, Lizbeth De La Cruz Santana, Margaret Smith, and Genevieve Tung. I'm also appreciative of constructive feedback about both my initial proposal and full manuscript from multiple anonymous reviewers.

Susan Buckley, my editor at MIT Press, heard coherence while I rambled at Pepita Coffee and coached necessary decisions when my curiosity overtook practicality. Thank you, Susan, for your discerning advice that greatly improved the vision and quality of this book.

My in-laws, Diane and Houston Flowers, oriented my travels along the Tubman Byway, graciously offered me the truck, and forgave my fumbles with that pesky shift cable.

I first used a computer because my mother brought her work home. Throughout the 1980s, mom schlepped me, my little sister, and an Apple IIe across town in a green VW Beetle. Mom—if there's an error in these pages, you'll let me know. I'm grateful for that, and your love.

Ade—while I wrote this book, you learned to read words like *the*, *we*, and *up*. Do you remember when we stapled your drawings together, creating books about the midnight zone, Pterygotus, and airplanes? What a pleasure nurturing you and your literacies.

And Ebony, coauthor of a most memorable journey. As a practical matter, were it not for your fellowship at Harvard's Radcliffe Institute for Advanced Study, our family wouldn't have enjoyed a magnificent year in Cambridge during which time I was able to run, read, and write with leisure. Over the years, I've benefitted from a unique privilege—witnessing you compose narratives lined with creativity and empathy. You've shown me why authors must avoid reductive caricature and thoughtfully represent people's fully realized lives. I've drawn from your expertise with the hope of shaping more complete and compassionate stories about how and why people make marks. Thanks for the Tubman Stamp, and for everything else, too.

1

OPENING REMARKS

You are an annotator. And so am I.

You are an annotator—just as you're a reader—who is familiar with acts of annotation. Annotators jot marginalia in books, use highlighters when reading, and add idiosyncratic signs of exclamation and confusion to dog-eared pages. Annotators, who once wrote names and dates on the verso of photographs, now tag friends in time-stamped images shared on social media. Annotators are cooks who modify recipe measurements next to lists of ingredients. Annotators are educators who mark papers, programmers who comment within code, data labelers who label data, and researchers who peer review. Annotators are artists who graffiti walls, influencers who hashtag posts, and parents who pencil their child's height and age on a doorjamb. While you may read "annotation" as an esoteric term or academic concern, I read this breadth of everyday activity as the visible and enduring expression of annotators. And, in this book, we will meet annotators who are educators and protestors, librarians and artists.

You are also an annotator who is well-versed with the social rhetoric of annotation. Chatting with friends, you *highlight* ideas, *underline* details, *underscore* fine points, or *gloss over* inconvenient facts. Anticipating a celebration, you remind someone to *mark* their calendar or *circle* the date. More formally, lawyers will argue that testimony be *struck from the record*, and lawmakers will hastily *rubber stamp* legislation. It isn't uncommon, even outside academic chatter, to hear someone *cite their sources*; the related social media meme declares, *show me the receipts*. You can name people who *left their mark* on an organization or the nation. Some people, in other circumstances, may leave *without a trace*. Your everyday exchanges are sprinkled with the idiomatic vocabulary of annotation.

And, as an annotator, you may now be wondering: Do I write in books? *Yes, I do*.

Should you write in books? *Probably*.

Can you write in this book? *Please!*

Yet how, and why, might you mark beyond these margins?

As an advocate of annotation, I am frequently asked by my students and colleagues: "Is it OK to write in a book?" Sometimes, the question is phrased to inquire about the relationship of annotation to literacy and learning: "When, and how, should students annotate what they read?"

It would be foolhardy to dismiss out of hand the meaningful marks of readers who, for centuries, have jotted marginalia across the pages of their books. "Annotations," writes Andrew Stauffer in *Book Traces*, "evince a culture of reading and book use whose features both recall our current social media exchanges (e.g., sharing, texting, liking, commenting on comments) and also seem part of a lost world."[1] Annotation permeates the literary record because the joy of reading is embodied and often includes this private-turned-social, and deeply resonant, practice of writing: "My notes transformed me," writes essayist Robert Rubsam, "from a passive reader into a thinker among other thinkers."[2] As annotators write in their books, thoughts of the mind are revealed by hand. Pages become waypoints of presence and response.

In recent years, the colloquial beauty of annotation has become a celebrated form in art and online. For Kameelah Janan Rasheed—an artist whose large text-based installations feature "overwriting" and emendation—building layers of annotation is a process of reflective visitation: "One of the things I often enjoy is going back and looking at things that I annotated years ago to see where my brain was. It is my old self meeting my current self."[3] Annotation is also a method for the artist Wendy Red Star, whose series *1880 Crow Peace Delegation* features handwritten historical details, humor, and speculative commentary added to nineteenth-century Crow chief portraits: "I'm also marking on history. And red—I always think about school and failing papers and getting that red mark on your paper. I wanted that red mark on history."[4] Online, communities of BookTube, Bookstagram, and BookTok readers curate social media that brims with videos showcasing annotators in action.[5] One Bowties & Books entry begins, "I thought it would be really freaking cool to annotate this book on camera."[6] In a YouTube video with over 168,000 views, BookTuber Melanie Diaz—better known as MelReads—is exuberant and playful in her assessment: "I love defacing books. What can I say. I'm just a monster by all intents and purposes. Maybe? Do I enjoy it? I do."[7]

Then again, annotation is anathema for some readers. Perhaps this is your opinion, too. Books mustn't be vandalized. Marginalia is graffiti and taboo, a transgressive act that defaces an object whose value is equivalent to its condition. This stance may be acute for those whose professional responsibilities uphold tacit conventions about common property. Moreover, annotation may be an unfamiliar practice for some readers because books are inaccessible, whether because of financial restriction or personal relevance. Debate about what constitutes readers' acceptable behavior in the margins—activity that is often dictated by institutions, like schools and libraries—can be usefully resolved "not by choosing one entrenched position or the other," suggests English professor Heather Jackson, "but by making an effort to understand the historical conditions that govern and have governed practices of annotation."[8]

This book is my effort to read histories of annotation and discern more participatory and just social futures written by the addition of notes to texts. In an era defined by social media and societal discord, this book examines how the norms and necessities of annotation have shifted amid new expressions of readership, agency, and critical literacy. And I will happily forgo further consideration about whether or not readers can write in this or that book because it's no longer useful to debate whether or not an annotator should. Such a provincial concern distracts from pressing political realities, etched across public settings like our schools and libraries, amidst what the American Library Association calls "a historic effort to ban and challenge materials that address racism, gender, politics, and sexual identity."[9] You have likely glimpsed fraught relationships among readers and texts, notes and norms that are contested and in revision—whether online, at school board meetings, or as displayed by place markers and symbols of the built environment. I am motivated to write about annotation as complementary to expansive visions of literacy, more critical approaches to learning, and creative efforts to rewrite public memory and social activism.

In my first book, I defined annotation simply, as a note added to a text.[10] Now, I write to survey the breadth of everyday texts and the multiplicity of inventive notes to further chart this genre's expressive possibility. Walking in a city, for example, you read walls perceived as canvases upon which murals and street art are added so passersby can comprehend context or a cause. Monuments, historical markers, statues, and signs are literal *landmarks*[11] that compose your connection to place and history; annotators who splatter paint, tag graffiti, or slap stickers onto these texts exhibit new traces of civic commentary. And the default features of our platform society have elevated acts of annotation—from quote tweets to hashtags and amended screenshots—as central to the taken-for-granted syntax of what makes your media social. This book is an invitation to rethink assumptions about textuality, authorship, and mark-makers as we reconsider how annotation is enmeshed in efforts to draft the liner notes of new educational and social arrangements. I venture to make visible a new social language of annotation that is read across time and texts, written across margins and contexts, and is collectively authored as critique and counternarrative.

Your engagement with *Re/Marks on Power* may benefit from knowing a bit more about me as an annotator. I am an annotator in the classroom where I regularly invite students to mark up course syllabi as they inquire about policies and readings, suggest changes to our assignments, and provide feedback about my decisions as an educator. In that context, my actions as an annotator invite students to contest my authority as a professor and reorient how power is negotiated within our course.[12] I am also an annotator across digital spaces where my public pedagogy has invited educators into online conversation about critical literacies and equitable learning. My leadership of the Marginal Syllabus project amplified, over the course of six years, social annotation as a form of public dialogue and a means by which educators pursued new professional learning pathways.[13] Occasionally, I am an annotator of Wikipedia, where my line edits—sometimes rejected by editors—recognize the agency of protestors who contest inherited relics by highlighting a monument with red paint or graffiti. I revise

OPENING REMARKS

entries if the verb "deface" honors object over objection, and I typically suggest a more appropriate term like "covered." And I have also been an annotator on the street, where the unearned protection of my appearance has allowed me to surreptitiously tag walls, affix stickers to signs, and creatively edit placemarks; I have done so anonymously for decades, without consequence. This book extends my justice-aligned praxis in synthesis with my educational, scholarly, and civic commitments as an annotator. I hope this book encourages your literacies as an annotator, too.

INSPIRATION

Here's one recent instance of annotation that inspired me to write *Re/Marks on Power*. It demonstrates how we encounter annotation in everyday environments, and how the marking of signs and symbols can alter our reading of history, memory, and place.

Muir Woods National Monument protects over five hundred acres of land, including an old-growth redwoods forest, and is located less than twenty miles north of San Francisco. Muir Woods staff, in collaboration with an interpretive team at the Golden Gate National Recreation Area, unveiled in 2021 an annotated sign that contextualizes local history and "provide[s] a learning opportunity to park visitors."[14] This annotation is not neutral and enables public pedagogy. An existing park placard labeled "Saving Muir Woods" was initially bedecked with yellow caution tape and a new laminated sign: "Alert: History Under Construction." Visitors were invited into social reading, and critical analysis, as they were informed: "Everything on this sign is accurate, but incomplete. The facts are not under construction, but the way we tell the history is."

This authoritative emendation of Muir Woods' history is intended to advance a more truthful and complex narrative for park visitors. The effort follows public "truth-telling" about John Muir's racist commentary,[15] as well as acknowledgment that "other white men involved in the conservation of Muir Woods also have problematic—though lesser-discussed—aspects of their legacies."[16] The original sign includes a Path to Preservation timeline that was modified with a more comprehensive set of facts presented like yellow sticky notes. Thanks to the practice and visibility of annotation, a sign once perceived as definitive approximated a working draft. Some of the

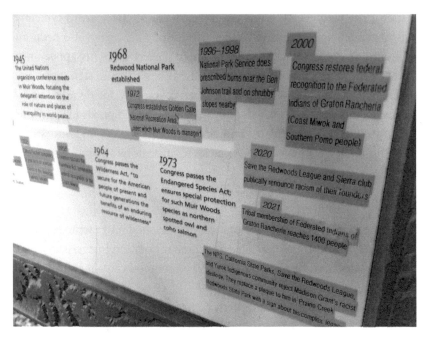

1.1 Original Path to Preservation timeline with labeled annotations at Muir Woods National Monument. Courtesy of Quinn Dombrowski.

annotated items "originally left out" of Muir Woods' origin story literally fill in timeline gaps, whereas other additions revise incomplete statements.

A new note labeled "Before European Contact" is the first of the timeline's nearly two dozen corrections and edits. It states: "20,000 Coast Miwok and Southern Pomo people, living at 850 sites, tend the lands of what is now Marin County and southern Sonoma County. Their prescribed burns care for the forest and their essential needs." A new 1861 note informs visitors: "Congress removes Indian title to almost all land in California. This action strips Coast Miwok people of title to their ancestral lands, of which Muir Woods is a part." Another new note, dated 1869, addresses Muir's racist writing: "John Muir refers to Indigenous people using racist language in his diary, later published, ignoring the genocide they survived. This contributes to an idea that Indigenous people don't belong in parks." Edited timeline notes also mention how Gifford Pinchot, first chief of the United States Forest Service, advocated for eugenics (1898), how women of color were excluded from the area's conservation efforts (1902), and

OPENING REMARKS

how the politician William Kent—who bought and donated the land that became Muir Woods National Monument—championed anti-Asian policy and rhetoric as with "California's Alien Land Laws . . . [that] prevent non-citizens from owning or leasing land . . . and create a more hostile environment for Asian immigrants in California" (1920).

One of the many park visitors who read this annotated sign was the educator and scholar Debbie Reese, who is an expert in the representation of Native and Indigenous peoples in children's literature. In 2019, Reese and I collaborated as part of the Marginal Syllabus project, and we've discussed annotation and critical literacy ever since. When I spoke with her about Muir Woods, she recalled the sign as a "wonderful intervention" that changed "my expectation of what someone at a park could do. Somebody there at the park made the decision to do that. Somebody is paying attention. And that is why it is so exciting."[17] The sign's annotation is a place-based tether connected to related information that Muir Woods staff also present online, as with commentary about the exclusion of women of color from conservation movements in the early 1900s[18] and Kent's efforts to prevent Asian immigration.[19] When the sign was first annotated, this land-marking was shared alongside a request for personal reflection because the "History Under Construction" note presented park visitors with two questions: "What do omissions in the historical narrative reveal about our society? How does knowing more shape your perspective on the past and the future?"

I read this annotation as social and justice-oriented activity. This public annotation enables critical historical analysis—and a way to teach truth—that stands in marked contrast to how accurate representations of history have been legislated out of school curricula. Indeed, I write at a moment of entrenched partisan debate in the US about public education and what historical facts and perspectives may be taught in school, how memory and cultural heritage is honored in civic settings, and whose identities and stories are sustained by our institutions.[20] Accordingly, and in Reese's assessment, Muir Woods' annotation "was inviting people to revisit, to pause, to rethink, and all of that is a tremendous plus."[21] And today, this landmark now displays the rewritten notes as a more accurate and enduring counternarrative. In 2022, the yellow notes were permanently added as a new feature of the redesigned Path to Preservation timeline. Muir Woods'

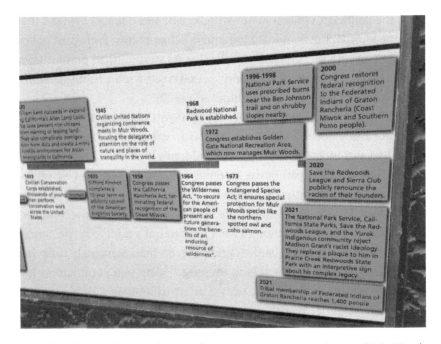

1.2 New Path to Preservation timeline incorporating annotations at Muir Woods National Monument. Courtesy of Quinn Dombrowski.

annotators rewrote provenance and place, and authored an opportunity for the public to connect the historical record with accessible entry points for discussions of truth and justice. Throughout *Re/Marks on Power*, we will read how the sociality and vitality of annotation shapes new narratives of public memory and belonging across learning environments.

REINTRODUCTION

This book is written about and for annotators whose marks are neither solitary nor disconnected from political concern. To do so, I call forth annotation as a social verb and document the meaningful participation of annotators implicated in vital educational and civic activities.[22] I also invite you to reevaluate how annotation has been—and can be—a collective act and accomplishment. What follows is my reintroduction to the social life of annotation.

First, the social life of annotation extends far beyond books and the constrained realm of reader marginalia. Within the humanities, scholarly interest in annotation is often affiliated with literary studies, the histories of books and the cultures of readership, as well as the investigations of archivists and medievalists. Contemporary annotation studies routinely examine books annotated from centuries past.[23] This small and helpful genre has detailed how annotators behave with books as material objects, the personal value of writing while reading, and how certain types of notes—as with dedications and messages to lovers—evince the social significance of readership. Without question, the most admired work in this area is Jackson's *Marginalia: Readers Writing in Books*. I concur with her assessment that "it is difficult to think of any kind of value attached to books that is not increased by the addition of notes."[24] Because of scholarship like Jackson's, we read about annotation as commonplace and enduring, and we can appreciate annotation as a conspicuous connection among reader and book, response and intellect. A present need, however, is to show mark-making with diverse tools and techniques, and as both multimodal and intertextual communication, especially as annotators collaboratively draft their social dreams. Annotation includes, yet also encompasses more than, marginalia jotted on a page, confined to the edges of a book, and cataloged in an archive. From digital media to our cityscapes, annotation must be acknowledged as a social accomplishment that transcends the printed page as annotators (re)inscribe meaning among their everyday spaces and discourses.

Second, the social life of annotation surpasses schooling and the limited purpose of academic performance. Research in the social sciences,[25] and specifically my field of education, has proven over decades that annotating texts does help students to learn.[26] This is the case for students in both grade and graduate school and who read both print and digital texts.[27] This is true for students who annotate fiction, poetry, and primary sources representing a range of academic disciplines.[28] And identifying these benefits is one aspect of my research, too.[29] Yet even when research examines the social affordances of annotation—as with students replying to peers, engaging with differing perspectives, and collaborating to make meaning of a text—there is an underlying and paradoxical assumption; learning is often presumed to be synonymous with mental processes that occur within the individual mind. Accordingly, annotation is commonly identified as the external expression—and empirical measure—of an individual student's effort (or "output"),[30] cognitive ability (or acquisition of "threshold concepts"),[31] and achievement (as with quiz scores and grades).[32] There is an atomistic tendency to reduce the scope of annotation to utilitarian skills, individual students with independent annotations, and discrete measures of academic achievement.

Unfortunately, research about annotation and learning has rarely deliberated, and has largely failed to fully account for, the fact "that the political forms and ends of learning matter and that seemingly neutral approaches to learning are never in fact neutral."[33] As I have written elsewhere, annotation is not neutral.[34] It is rare that inquiry about annotation is brought into conversation with the political dimensions of learning, much less the political moment. One noteworthy exception is my prior work with colleagues in the Marginal Syllabus—a project that promoted educators' justice-directed learning—and our efforts to study, for over six years, how we made "viable opportunities to leverage the critical and social qualities of annotation for more equitable literacy education across online and on-the-ground contexts."[35] Nevertheless, more must be done to study annotation as a social verb and call it forth as eclipsing individual reasoning and didactic reader response. Within a broadened vision of literacy learning, annotation can be written, read, and studied as a collective endeavor whose traces help contest relations of power and narrate justice-centered futures.

And third, we can also trace the social life of annotation among place-based marks that are responsive to and layered atop our daily surroundings as land-marks. Acts of annotation mark texts and materials that are situated across, and also comprised of, everyday natural and built environments. As scholar Shannon Mattern observes in *Code and Clay, Data and Dirt*, place is "legible"; when land and other features of locale become marked, as people do for various official and idiosyncratic reasons, landmarks punctuate place. From historical place markers alongside country roads to murals adorning building façades, "our physical landscapes inscribe, transmit, and even embody information—about their histories, their state of repair, their potential uses, and so forth."[36] Annotators' land-marking—of walls, signs,

1.3 Indigenous Sign Initiative installation marking a stop sign on land that, today, is also referred to as the Clayton neighborhood of Denver. Photograph by author (2023).

placards, posts, barricades, billboards, mailboxes, newsstands, gates, columns, bridges, fences, windows, statues, stairwells, doorways, stalls, arches, awnings, trash cans, recycling bins, electrical boxes, and much more—communicates a means of place-making that (re)shapes attributes of the environment into legible texts. Over time, these disrupted texts surface new notes and narratives, as with artist Gregg Deal's Indigenous Sign Initiative that repurposes "the unassuming utilitarian design of street signs [to] create confrontation, a statement of recognition and garner an entry point to understanding the simple but important statement that these are Native lands."[37] Historian John Stilgoe suggests a useful analogy for understanding annotation as place-based land-marking: "The built environment is a sort of palimpsest, a document in which one layer of writing has been scraped off, and another one applied. An acute, mindful explorer who holds up the palimpsest to the light sees something of the earlier message, and a careful, confident explorer of the built environment soon sees all sorts of traces of past generations."[38] We encounter the social life of annotation when reading landmarks and comprehending, amid layered notes, how annotators mark their built environments as a local ledger of public discourse and memory.

DEFINITION

As an annotator, three arguments ground my rationale for redefining the possibilities of annotation. First, as we saw at Muir Woods, annotation is more than book marginalia. From textbooks to town squares to TikTok, annotation manifests as a hybrid act producing divergent marks that thrive outside the tightly bound pages of a book. Second, the social life of annotation is as important as individual reader response. Annotation must be studied and promoted as a social endeavor coauthored by groups of mark-makers, with interactive media, spanning on-the-ground and online settings, and in response to shared commitments. Third, annotation is a critical practice; it is an essential act that inscribes struggles for justice and social change. Annotation should be embraced as exemplifying, and helping to extend through embodied and digital spaces, a critical literacy lineage through which annotators—including learners in school—read and write words so as to critique and change their worlds.

My three arguments about annotation—as critical and in dialogue with (in)justice, as hybrid and thriving beyond book marginalia in everyday settings, and as social and privileging civic activity rather than private response—encompass an intent to reintroduce and represent annotation as the creative, communal, and essential expression of readers-as-writers. These arguments also make clear my stance toward literacy and learning and how I understand what it means to learn and participate in literacy practices. In their book *Living Literacies*, Kate Pahl and Jennifer Rowsell show us how literacies are "historically situated sets of social practices that are highly dependent on what people *do* with literacy."[39] Annotators do annotation and, as I document, this literacy practice is associated with many sources and spaces beyond printed books. Consequently, educators who read this book might reconsider referencing a broader repertoire of everyday texts for students to read, annotate, and discuss, including historical records, walls, monuments, social media, and landmarks. Furthermore, because annotation is a social practice that facilitates peer collaboration

OPENING REMARKS

and negotiated meaning, we should help learners, including classroom teachers, rewrite reader response when authoring annotation about their academic and everyday interests.[40] And because annotation is a critical practice enabling critique and contextualization, we can promote the shared addition of notes to texts as annotators craft counternarratives. The creative possibilities of annotation are apparent and relevant to learners' lives, as well as their critical literacies and civic activities.

I write about the critical, hybrid, and civic qualities of annotation because literacy and learning practices reflect power. How does access to material resources shape the types of notes people add to texts? Whose knowledge is welcomed and celebrated when texts are annotated? And in what ways does annotation reveal valued cultural practices and social dreams? This book spans contexts, from literacy education to participatory politics, as I chronicle how the annotation of everyday texts is a confluence of authority and resistance, an amalgam of agency and imagination. It has been over two hundred years since the term "marginalia" appeared as a neologism, and well over a millennium since Roman emperors and their handwritten *annotatio* remarked on rulings and imperial power.[41] Given shifting conceptions of literacy and learning, and in a moment of deep concern about equitable schooling and society, it is time for a fresh read and rewrite of annotation. For centuries, scholars have both written and studied what Jackson categorized as three "basic particles" of historical annotation: glosses that translate and explain terminology; rubrics that mark headings and index sections; and scholia that comment on and contextualize a primary source.[42] To this set I add a contemporary form: *re/marks*.

I work, through this book, to recast annotation as implicated in peoples' meaningful and socially vital activities, as woven into multimodal texts and cultural contexts, and as mediated by everyday language and power. To do so, I propose the concept of re/marks, which I define as annotation traces collectively read and (re)written so as to advance counternarratives and more just social futures. This term makes prominent the inherent hybridity and visual assertiveness of annotation as both a textual disruption and social intervention. As for the scope of re/marks, you may read my emphasis on "more just social futures" as an untoward aspiration for something as seemingly unremarkable as annotation. Indeed, our ability to follow annotation traces over texts and time does not indicate an achievement of social justice. Rather, my intent is to show that the actions of annotators are legible, longstanding, and instructive amidst the ongoing project of shaping a pluralistic society that values equality and affirms human dignity. My original concept is a useful heuristic for demonstrating how people's recursive marks have highlighted, literally and metaphorically, the continued struggle against social inequality and oppressive ideology. And my research will show that those who closely read everyday symbols and spaces, and who then compose additive responses of resistance and imagination, are annotators—for their pursuit of more just social futures has been visualized through traces we can call annotation.

In defining re/marks, my use of "traces" is also intentional. Anthropologist Tim Ingold suggests that a trace is "any enduring mark left in or on a solid surface by a continuous movement."[43] Traces, according to Ingold, are either additive or reductive, though what manifests as an *enduring* mark should be clarified in light of our interest in annotation. Book marginalia may fade, especially if written in pencil. Sticky notes become unstuck. Wheat paper disintegrates and falls from a wall. Murals are whitewashed. And spray paint weathers or may be blasted with water, though faint echoes of graffiti can still broadcast meaning. I don't consider "enduring" to be synonymous with permanence; rather, enduring suggests qualities of sustained and legible presence. An "enduring mark left in or on a solid surface" is neither fixed nor immutable. Traces can be read, and they may also be re-marked or redacted—whether by other annotators, changes to the environment, or simply due to the passage of time. You may not always encounter a given trace in an unaltered state. And whenever you read this book, it's likely that some annotations I analyze will have changed or disappeared; as we'll read in chapter 3, I experienced that impermanence, too. My definition of re/marks privileges glimpsed visibility—not perpetuity— of a collective literacy practice, as marks read and rewritten inscribe new social narratives.

INQUIRY

I acknowledge there is no fixed method for identifying and writing about re/marks. The purpose of my book isn't to model a procedure or report findings from a discrete study of annotation. Rather, I am presenting a new argument about how to read the histories and literacies of annotation. My inquiry was exploratory as I enacted a core set of personal and scholarly values to honor how annotators compose and comprehend justice-centered narratives.

I selected four cases to present re/marks and broaden how annotation is represented in the research literature. Doing so required that I question whose voices to privilege and whose expertise to prioritize. You will find that I center stories and social concerns, feature examples and images, and credit people intentionally marginalized or inadvertently disassociated with annotation scholarship. I listened to and learned from artists, park rangers, classroom teachers, librarians, authors, curators, and fellow academics. Some were colleagues I've known for years, while others replied graciously to an email; everyone interviewed for this project reviewed their contributions prior to publication. One productive use of my privilege was amplifying the perspectives and practices of these annotators. My efforts did include some methods familiar to more traditional studies of annotation. I visited historical archives and cultural institutions where I viewed centuries-old documents to then analyze primary sources. I did so cognizant of archival absences, of truths silenced by and erased from official records, for "power permeates every aspect of the archival endeavor."[44] Overlooked archive traces are featured prominently in my second and third chapters, as well as at the beginning of chapter 4, to underscore the value of historicity and archival inquiry when studying critical literacy. And, as you will see, I complemented my interviews and archival study with literature from multiple disciplines. While annotation is a literacy practice, I followed discussions of mark-making across many fields including history, architecture, literature, cartography, geography, art history, library and information science, and education. My cases also benefit from activists, journalists, and visual artists who have publicly recorded and shared their annotations, too.

To research re/marks, it was crucial that I close my computer and walk away from my desk. I drove hundreds of miles along the Eastern Shore, retracing Harriet Tubman's footsteps through Maryland, Delaware, and Pennsylvania along a byway that bears her name and celebrates stories of self-emancipation. I walked through security checkpoints, stationed by armed guards, at the Library of Congress in Washington, DC, and at the San Ysidro Port of Entry that connects San Diego and Tijuana along the US–Mexico border. I visited parks, museums, public squares, and many libraries, and I traveled along both the Pacific and Atlantic coasts. I conducted fieldwork—and I moved among constructed and contested margins—because enduring marks appear as a result of continuous movement. The visible traces of mobility are valuable to the study of everyday literacies, like annotation, as education scholars observe how "materials, persons, practices, and texts are dynamically configured across varied temporalities and spaces."[45] My curiosity about page and place compelled me to locate, read, and represent re/marks as inscribed with words in our world.

Another method that I carefully practiced was citation. As noted, I interviewed annotators who have accented narratives that reveal societal injustice and suggest alternative futures. And I reference primary sources, archival materials, projects, and art seldom read as relevant to the conventional repertory of annotation studies. I have a social responsibility to model a more critical use of annotation within *Re/Marks on Power*. One way of doing so is through my citational practice. Scholarly references are annotation. A citation—when added by an author to their text, and so as to substantiate a claim or indicate an alternative view—is the addition of a note to a text. And citation, as a practice reflecting both individual bias and the rigid boundaries of institutionalized knowledge, is also a political choice that reinscribes and redirects power.[46] While discussing how traces of annotations help compose more just social futures, it is prudent that I discuss how such a process also informed the production of this book. This is one additional way for me, as an annotator, to rewrite and reorient re/marks of annotation while advancing efforts that some researchers call "citational justice."[47]

My citational practice is influenced, in part, by scholar Sara Ahmed and her policy from *Living a Feminist Life* in which she does not cite any white men.[48] She recognizes that citations "are the materials through which, from which, we create our dwellings."[49] Across academic disciplines, dwellings that shelter the scholarship of annotation are overwhelmingly white, male, and associated with the Western canon, echoing English professor Stauffer's observation that "most of the critical and historical work on these traces [marginalia] has focused on medieval and early modern readers and their books."[50] For instance, the 1991 volume *Annotation and Its Texts* includes chapters exclusively authored by white men from the US and Europe. Jackson's celebrated *Marginalia: Readers Writing in Books* examines "annotators in the English-speaking world during the past three centuries;"[51] the ten-page index catalogs mostly white men and their work from bygone eras. I also reject a choice to discuss "the margins," whether from rhetorical or psychological perspectives, and then center the histories and ideas of white scholars.[52]

To resist and rework these citational trends, I learned from scholars Catherine D'Ignazio and Lauren Klein, whose book *Data Feminism* discloses citation metrics and honestly confronts the challenges of reproducing bias through citation. D'Ignazio and Klein mention both the benefits and limitations of quantifying citations that represent values in action, as they transparently audited "[their] citations and the examples that [they] elevate in the book."[53] I've adapted their methods with respect to racial and gender representation: Of the 337 individuals named and referenced in this book—including historical figures, political leaders, scholars, journalists, artists, educators, and others—48 percent are people of color (including 1 percent who also publicly identify as trans or non-binary), 27 percent are white women, 24 percent are white men (and of these individuals, over one-third are long-departed politicians and military officers), and 1 percent are white individuals who publicly identify as trans or non-binary.[54] As a white male annotator, and as a scholar who advocates for critical literacy and learning, I have attempted to enact a more just citational practice throughout this book that resists—per Ahmed's metaphor—prevailing academic "materials" and begins to modestly build a more equitable and inclusive "dwelling" for the future scholarship of annotation.

STRUCTURE

Re/Marks on Power includes six chapters: this introduction, four cases about justice-centered annotation, and a conclusion about the theory, practice, and promise of re/marks. The examples throughout this book reflect my scholarly interests and personal biases. Additionally, my close reading of annotation is rooted by proximal dissonances among American history, politics, and education relevant to my students and colleagues. There are, undoubtedly, compelling instances of re/marks in other cultural and historical contexts; I hope that readers outside of North America come to understand why I have limited the geographic and political scope of this book.

In chapter 2, "Her Mark," I examine public recognition and remembrance of Harriet Tubman. I begin with the 1874 Congressional Record—the first of many documented efforts to secure her military pension following the Civil War—through to our present day and commemorative traces observable in American iconography and public memory. Annotation, as I show, is a novel and meaningful way to discern how marks associated with Tubman's achievements have persisted for well over a century. In the case of her incomparable life, this common literacy practice has accompanied: bureaucracy, as Tubman petitioned the Bureau of Pensions and officials processed her claim; banknote, as with current efforts to print the Tubman twenty; and byway, as her name graces a rural route that retraces the Underground Railroad. I share an original analysis of Tubman's annotated pension file, I stamp Tubman twenties in a used books store, and I travel the Tubman Byway across three Mid-Atlantic states. I also present what is likely the first scholarly discussion of Harriet Tubman's handwritten marks. Though perceived by many as illiterate, I show Tubman as a conscientious annotator for "her mark" expressed multiple literacies as she sought rightful recompense for her military services.

Chapter 3, "Marking Boundaries," concerns the annotated border between Mexico and the US. In 1848, at the end of the Mexican–American War, this international boundary was ruled as a line atop a map. I first analyze annotations added to the Treaty of Guadalupe Hidalgo, focusing on the annotated and the imprecisely traced treaty map that delimited the boundary between San Diego and Tijuana. I then review how this contested border was marked across the borderlands during two nineteenth-century binational surveys whose commissioners, engineers, and laborers added 276 monuments along the line. Among these land-marks is Monument No. 258, a towering obelisk, with the legacy of cooperation and division carved into its four marble faces. I visited Monument No. 258 at Playas de Tijuana, where it is overshadowed by America's hostile border wall and an even taller surveillance tower. I describe how annotators have transformed the wall at Playas de Tijuana with the addition of mariposa, graffiti, hashtags, names, and three prominent murals—Mural de la Hermandad, the Deported Veterans Mural Project, and the Playas de Tijuana Mural Project. This marked margin is far more nuanced than partisan rhetoric or dispassionate policy suggest, and we will glimpse that complexity thanks to the persistence of emended maps, monuments, and murals.

In chapter 4, "Marked Men," I survey America's memorial landscape to discuss how marks added to public monuments demonstrate communities reading the past and rewriting hateful ideology. I begin with blood and red ink thrown on the Confederate statue Silent Sam and review a legacy of University of North Carolina students defacing this monument prior to its removal. This example helps me distinguish history from memory, and I argue that an annotated monument publicly communicates and makes visible that distinction. I then introduce the literacy act of *figurative highlighting* to describe how public monuments are marked during street protests. I illustrate this concept with examples from recent racial justice uprisings, as with projections that highlighted the Robert E. Lee Monument in Richmond, Virginia. I also scrutinize the limitations of *contextualization*, a strategy whereby new interpretive resources augment problematic monuments to assuage contemporary concerns. The failings of such annotation are apparent in the example of the Equestrian Statue of Theodore Roosevelt once located at the American Museum of Natural History in New York City. This chapter concludes with acts of monumental creativity. I speak with an elementary school teacher in New Orleans whose third-grade students responded to the 2017 removal of four Confederate monuments by self-publishing a book that reimagined the city's memorial landscape.

Chapter 5, "Book Marks," concerns the celebrated middle grade novel *Melissa* by Alex Gino and their #SharpieActivism campaign to correct the book's title using annotation. Published in 2015, *Melissa* remains one of the most frequently banned books in America, and I first discuss how #SharpieActivism—and public support of transgender youth and LGBTQIA+ representation in literature—coincides with recent book censorship efforts. My analysis of #SharpieActivism focuses on a singular group of annotators—public and school librarians who creatively interpreted and shared book marks within the familiar literacy setting of the library. To appreciate librarians' participation in #SharpieActivism, I review how libraries classify and mark books with call numbers and how the bibliographic classification of books about gender and sexuality reflects harmful and heteronormative ideology. In this context, I then interpret #SharpieActivism as a queer intervention and suggest that the marking of *Melissa* extends critical librarianship efforts. I analyze social media posts by public libraries, including Twitter and Instagram posts, as well as TikTok videos, to explain how annotated copies of *Melissa* circulated affirming LGBTQIA+ counternarratives. And my chapter concludes with the public pedagogy of school librarians who joined #SharpieActivism and annotated *Melissa* with and for their students as an opportunity to remark on trans pride and justice.

"Ma(r)king Narratives," my conclusion in chapter 6, retraces re/marks across cases to build a broader conceptual argument reimagining annotation as a familiar yet transformative literacy practice. Drawing together my commentary about Harriet Tubman's legacy, the US–Mexico border, America's memorial landscape, and #SharpieActivism, I first suggest that annotation be written and read as critical literacy; in doing so, I discuss why it's important to discern enduring re/marks as both resistance to injustice and evidence that indignity may be redressed. Second, I argue that annotation be understood as an inherently hybrid literacy and that we can view the syncretism of this social act as it spans cultural and discursive contexts. And third, I contend that annotation be perceived as civic literacy and that we recognize the persistence of notes added to public compositions that advance justice-directed counternarratives. As a complement to this conceptual perspective, I also identify four concrete suggestions for how annotators—of various ages, and across both civic and educational settings—can respond to marks of injustice, often collaboratively and publicly, with re/marks of resistance and creativity. Annotators' mark-making tools and methods are often simple and accessible, and I hope my concluding comments help you to better notice, comprehend, and contribute annotation that can alter ordinary texts and (re)orient everyday contexts toward more just social futures.

I write this book in gratitude to annotators, many of whom are marginalized or unknown, whose marks are often unattributed or excluded from annotation scholarship and colloquial recognition. Perhaps this includes you, too. And I am eager to share this book with students, educators, librarians, and scholars who are ready to reassess annotation by reconsidering its definition, location, and function. I write for readers-turned-annotators who cherish the nexus of text and context, word and world, the social scribes among us keen to question how annotation has and can be composed, and who are eager to mark both their books and public discourses. My hope is that *Re/Marks on Power* helps you reimagine traces tethered to texts and also reinvigorates annotation as a critical, hybrid, and civic literacy practice that transforms notes into sociopolitical narratives.

We are annotators who can enliven the histories and literacies of annotation with justice-centered narratives. Mark my words.

2

HER MARK

We are annotators who can follow marks of public recognition and remembrance.

Nine years after the end of the Civil War, on June 22, 1874, the United States Congress' Committee on War Claims filed *Report No. 787*. It accompanied House of Representatives Bill 3786 to support "the relief of Harriet Tubman."[1] Despite prior petition, Tubman had received inadequate compensation for her three years of military service—from May of 1862 through January of 1865—as a Union Army scout, nurse, and spy.[2] To date, she had secured just $200 for her role as a scout.[3] The record of testimony in Report No. 787 includes an annotation: "I approve fully Colonel Montgomery's estimate of the value of Harriet Tubman's services." The annotator was Brigadier-General Rufus Saxon, and he had annotated the back of a letter received from Colonel James Montgomery. Report No. 787 is unambiguous about the location and purpose of Saxon's annotation—"on the back of this letter is indorsed"—and also quotes Montgomery's initial assessment that Tubman was "a most remarkable colored woman and valuable as a scout. I am well acquainted with her character and actions for several years past."

Harriet Tubman's work with Colonel Montgomery is irrefutable and was, according to historian Nell Irvin Painter, "unusual for a woman."[4] It was Tubman who, in 1863, aided Montgomery and 150 members of the

Second South Carolina Volunteers—an infantry regiment of free and formerly enslaved Black men—during the successful and now-famous raid on Combahee Ferry.[5] This raid was the first major American military operation planned and executed by a woman. The 1874 report "establishes conclusively the fact that [Tubman's] services in the various capacities of nurse, scout, and spy were of great service and value to the Government." Because of Report No. 787, the Committee on War Claims recommended "the sum of $2,000 for services rendered by her to the Union Army." Yet despite evidence, including Saxon's annotated endorsement of Montgomery's letter, H.R. Bill 3786 passed the House but was dismissed by the Senate.[6]

This single annotation, this instance of endorsement and evidence ignored, foreshadowed indignities that Harriet Tubman would endure as she sought to secure recognition of—and rightful recompense for—her military services. For over 150 years, written records have detailed Tubman's accomplishments as conductor on the Underground Railroad, abolitionist, suffragist, matriarch, and American icon. Amid this documentation is annotation, or notes added to texts. We will consider these notes as re/marks that trace Tubman's ordeals and also extend narratives of meaning that signal her ongoing significance. This corpus of serendipity reverberates across texts and time given contemporary concern for power and justice. And, starting with Saxon's note, we will follow a trail of annotation that connects struggles to secure Tubman's military pension with today's efforts to memorialize her legacy in public memory.

But why do so, given the extensive bibliographic record established by historians? Because we are advocates of learning and literacy and should uplift this recent appreciation of Harriet Tubman by historian Kate Clifford Larson: "Tubman had great *literacy*. Her education, borne out of self-preservation necessitated by extreme oppression, consisted of learning to read the night sky, the rivers, streams and marshes, woods, and fields. She could read people and discern character. Those tools, those *literacies*, shaped her intellect, nurturing a genius that fomented incredible change."[7] Because our review of various texts, with careful attention to attendant notes, will explain how public narratives about Tubman have been documented, debated, and also (dis)regarded. Annotation has functioned as evidence, evaluation, and authority when recognizing and recalling her legacy. Because, as we will see, small yet unmistakable traces readily locate a synergy of everyday expression and enduring power. And because the deliberate marking of texts tangibly effects context, for annotation about Tubman has contributed to social action and change. Re/marks will be analyzed as participatory and public and we will meet annotators who have coauthored counternarrative and remembrance. Tubman's legacy will orient our curiosity to the nexus of text, note, context, and narrative and is one response to "demand [for] deeply researched, purposeful and respectful interpretation, not 'gilded haze,' to reveal the true story of this remarkable woman."[8]

"A DOUBLE CLAIM" DENIED

More than a decade after Report No. 787 was disregarded, the Dependent and Disability Pension Act of June 27, 1890, established a new system of pension benefits for Civil War veterans, their widows, and their children. Historian Larson's analysis of records from Tubman's pension file[9] shows that "within a month of the enactment of the act in June 1890, Tubman filed her first claim; five years later, on October 16, 1895, she was finally granted an $8-per-month pension as the widow of Nelson Davis."[10] Davis, who was also known as Nelson Charles and, like Tubman, self-emancipated, had served in Company G of the 8th US Colored Volunteer Infantry during the Civil War. He was Tubman's second husband and died in 1888 after nineteen years of marriage together in Auburn, New York.

To receive a widow's pension, the act of 1890 required that Tubman provide proof of Davis' death and his honorable discharge from the military, certify they had been married prior to the enactment of the act, and prove that she was "without other means of support than her daily labor."[11] For five years, Tubman and her pension attorney Orin McCarty submitted to the US Bureau of Pensions various forms, records, depositions, and affidavits. And as the bureau received these documents, each was annotated— always with stamps and sometimes with handwritten evaluations. At the time, these annotations verified how Tubman met pension criteria. In retrospect, we can review the notes as an injurious record of doubt made visible by laborious processes of bureaucracy.

The 111 pages of documents that comprise Tubman's pension file include hundreds of annotations—marginalia, insertions, deletions, handwritten signatures, stamped signatures, checkmarks, codes, fragments of paper taped to forms, stamps in a half dozen colors of ink, and the processual glosses of bureaucrats and archivists. I have identified a group of fourteen that are distinct. All of these re/marks were written in pencil: "death 1st husband," "marriage," "no divorce," "no means of support but labor, no re-marriage," "comrade identity." All were added to the lower left corner of various documents by annotators within the Bureau of Pensions.[12] The first of these annotations was "death," added to Nelson Davis' Record of Death and accompanied by the stamp "US Pension Office A Jul 24 1890." The last of these penciled notes was "no prior services," added to the affidavit of Charles Peterson, a neighbor who testified that "Nelson Davis had not been in the military or naval service prior to about Sept 1863." This section of Peterson's testimony was also underlined in red. The affidavit was stamped "US Pension Office H Jan 10 1895."

These fourteen annotations trace another of Tubman's many journeys—one that culminated thirty years after the end of the Civil War and in spite of her own military service—so she could receive $8 per month as a widow.[13] And, according to historian Donald Shaffer's study of soldiers and widows who successfully obtained Civil War pensions, Tubman was fortunate: "Inequality in pensions stemmed from the special disadvantages African Americans experienced in the application process and the racism and misbehavior of important players in the adjudication of their claims. In other words, racial discrimination in the Civil War pension system was de facto rather than de jure in nature."[14] Collectively, these fourteen annotations substantiate broader observations about "biased pension examiners and documentation rules"[15] encountered by African American Civil War veterans and further suggest that we should not separate procedural marks from prejudicial re/marks.

Though now pensioned, literal and figurative commentary about Tubman did not end in 1895. "Many would have expected Harriet Tubman to savor the moment," writes historian Catherine Clinton, for "she owned her own home and now had a small but steady income to maintain her household. She was nearly seventy years old and had surely earned the right to retire from the challenging pace she had undertaken since her return from war. But this was never Tubman's style."[16] Furthermore, various styles of annotation would help narrate her life for years to come.

2.1 Annotations added by Bureau of Pensions officials to four documents that Harriet Tubman submitted to support her claim for a widow's pension: "marriage" added to a letter from the Central Presbyterian Church of Auburn, July 15, 1890 (Tubman Pension File, 13), upper left; "no means of support but labor, no re-marriage" added to affidavit of Henry Lucas and Maggie Lucas, July 15, 1890 (Tubman Pension File, 40), upper right; "no divorce" added to affidavit of William Stewart, October 13, 1894 (Tubman Pension File, 31), lower right; "comrade identity" added to affidavit of Dorsey Brainard, October 16, 1894 (Tubman Pension File, 29), lower left. National Archives.

Harriet Tubman continued fighting to receive her own military pension. And annotations complemented her cause. There are struck-through sections and line edits on an 1898 claim "against the U.S." that Tubman submitted to Congress for $1,800. Testifying, yet again, to her pension attorney, Tubman described "three years service as a nurse and cook in hospitals, and as commander of several men (eight or nine) as scouts during the late war of the Rebellion."[17] Three words were underlined for emphasis: "Eighteen hundred dollars." This affidavit was accompanied by a petition, also sent to Congress in 1898, that stated: "We the undersigned residents of the city of Auburn N.Y. Earnestly request you to call up the claim of Harriet Tubman (now Harriet Davis) . . . [t]he claim for her personal valuable services to the government during the late war of the rebellion as Scout nurse and Spy."[18] Coincidentally, three words were also underlined: "Scout," "nurse," and "Spy." The fifty-eight petitioners—including prominent suffragists, philanthropists, and one former member of the House of Representatives—were annotators whose inscriptions added cumulative concern to their legal appeal. Despite this support, Tubman's request for deserved recompense remained ignored.

In February of 1899, after years of struggle, a Special Act of Congress increased Harriet Tubman's pension to $20 per month. A month earlier, H.R. Bill 4982—which sought to "place upon the pension roll of the United States the name Harriet Tubman Davis, late a nurse in the United States Army, and pay her a pension at the rate of twenty-five dollars per month"[19]—had advanced to the Senate along with H.R. Report 1774 from the Committee on Invalid Pensions.[20] That report included the very quote from Colonel Montgomery previously featured as evidence in 1874. It further noted: "This woman has a double claim on the Government. She went into the field and hospitals and cared for the sick and wounded. She saved lives. In her old age and poverty a pension of $25 per month is none too much."

Yet, once again, the Senate disagreed with the House's recommendation. *Senate Report No. 1619* reduced Tubman's proposed pension to $20 a month by combining her current $8 rate as a widow with an additional $12 for her service as a nurse.[21] The Senate report stated: "The number of nurses on the pension roll at a rate higher than $12 per month is very few indeed."[22] The Special Act signed by President McKinley on February 28 is notable for what it erased from the record, as it authorized the Secretary of the Interior "to place on the pension roll . . . the name of Harriet Tubman Davis, widow of Nelson Davis, late a private in Company G, Eighth Regiment United States Colored Infantry, and pay her a pension at the rate of twenty dollars per month in lieu of what she is now receiving." Tubman's "double claim" was denied.

Annotations, again, evidence the erasure of Tubman's military service and reaffirmed her status as a widow. By March 23, 1899, the final version of Tubman's Widow's Pension form had been reviewed and approved by officials at the Bureau of Pensions. While Tubman's plight securing her pension is often cited by scholars and biographers, her 1899 Widow's Pension form is glossed over and seldom discussed, prompting my original archival analysis; indeed, I have not seen this marked document reproduced in any contemporary biography of Tubman. This form, an annotated artifact, deserves greater recognition and scrutiny given our concern for the addition of re/marks to the historical record.

Notes added to Harriet Tubman's 1899 Widow's Pension form were likely written by four different annotators on account of the various scripts, handwritten emendations, and ink. The words "Special Act" were added in large red cursive above the form's title, designating a new header. A smaller note, written by the same person and inserted below the title, reads "reissue to [illegible] widow of soldier & pensioner & allow under Special Act." That red annotation, however, has been mostly crossed-through, written over and corrected by another, in thicker black ink, each word underlined for emphasis: "under general law by special act." The soldier's name is listed as "Nelson Davis alias Nelson Charles," though an annotator obscured "alias Nelson Charles" with gray curlicue. The form does not indicate when the widow's pension will terminate, though the annotator writing in red cursive has added another interlinear note: "In lieu of certificate dated October 16, 1895." Other annotations accompany detail about the claimant and soldier, as with various letters, the certificate number "415288," a stamped "S.," and the city "Buffalo."

Of the many marks added to Tubman's Widow's Pension form, one is conclusive and damning. Notice the marginal note written vertically along the right side of the form in neat black cursive: "Claimant pensioned as Harriet Davis widow of Nelson Davis alias Nelson Charles." That re/mark was an assertion of power and patriarchy. It is further proof that Tubman was "denied an earned pension because of her gender."[23] Tubman would receive a $20 per month widow's pension until her death on March 10, 1913.

THE "TUBMAN TWENTY"

One hundred and three years later, on April 20, 2016, Secretary of the Treasury Jacob Lew announced that the Obama Administration would begin the process of redesigning American currency so as to "highlight democracy in action and reflect the diversity of our great nation."[24] Secretary Lew's most noteworthy pronouncement was "that for the first time in more than a century, the front of our currency will feature the portrait of a woman—Harriet Tubman on the $20 note."[25] Whenever the "Tubman twenty" is eventually printed, most likely in 2030, it will have already been marked by the legacy and social life of annotation.

2.2 Harriet Tubman's annotated Widow's Pension form, March 23, 1899. National Archives.

Historian Clarence Lusane's recent book *Twenty Dollars and Change: Harriet Tubman and the Ongoing Fight for Racial Justice and Democracy* recalls how the Tubman twenty was devised and also celebrated, debated, and criticized.[26] Briefly, a grassroots effort during Obama's presidency influenced the Treasury's currency redesign process, which was then postponed by the Trump Administration and restarted by President Biden.[27] As Lusane recounts, critique has come from across the political spectrum and among Black communities, because there is "principled dispute regarding whether including her image on the twenty honors or exploits the integrity of her life and legacy."[28] For example, professor Brittney Cooper, a women and gender studies scholar, emphasizes the interconnectedness of symbols, systems, and change: "If Tubman is going to be linked to conversations on capital, that conversation must be about a redistribution and funneling of resources and money into Black communities . . . We don't need America to put Black women on its money. We need America to put its money on Black women."[29] Tubman's fight for her pension—characterized by the government's decades-long inaction, a reduction of monthly payment despite her "double claim," and ultimate refusal to recognize her military service—is unmistakably echoed by Cooper's advocacy. Lusane, however, concludes without ambiguity: "Winning the Tubman twenty represents a small but important victory over the pervasive symbolism of white male America and the marginalization of people of color, women, and those who have always been othered."[30]

Amidst public debate over the Tubman twenty, research about "the representational shortcomings of American currency" connects this timely decision with acts of historical annotation. Legal scholars Genevieve Tung and Ruth Anne Robbins explain how "the manner for designing federal paper money has been characterized by arbitrary and arguably autocratic decision-making and resistance to open processes that consider the creativity and insights of the public."[31] And that is the case for the $20 banknote. An arbitrary and autocratic choice placed President Jackson's portrait on the bill. Annotations reveal that decision. But for a few handwritten re/marks, scrawled in pencil atop a 1927 Department of the Treasury memo, President Grover Cleveland would grace the $20 note. Tung and Robbins recall in detail the machinations of statutory authority associated with currency portraiture. A century ago, only Secretary of the Treasury Andrew Mellon

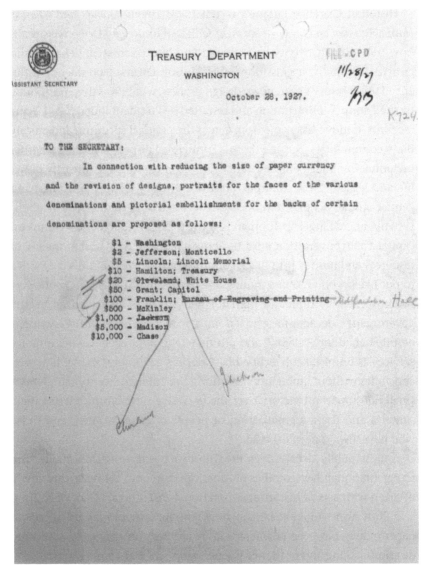

2.3 Treasury Department memo regarding paper currency portraits, with handwritten annotations, October 28, 1927. National Archives.

had the "ultimate authority" to annotate such a memo. Secretary Mellon was most likely the annotator who crossed through President Cleveland's name and inserted "Jackson," while also striking President Jackson's placement on the $1,000 note to be replaced with "Cleveland."

The last comprehensive redesign of American currency culminated in 1929. At the time, annotations helped place President Jackson on the $20 note. Today, the Treasury Department is yet again redesigning currency. As we anticipate Harriet Tubman's face on the twenty, additional representational re/marks continue to make visible her legacy.

In the fall of 2021, I visited Kilgore Books in downtown Denver. Kilgore is a funky, beloved used books store known for its comics, zines, local art, and snug charm. I was never a regular, though I visited a handful of times when living in the city. While conducting research for this book, I wasn't surprised to see Kilgore named among a dozen Stamping Stations listed on the Tubman Stamp website.[32] The Tubman Stamp was created by artist Dano Wall in 2017 as a DIY response to the Trump Administration suspending the $20 banknote redesign process. Wall used a laser cutter to engrave rubber for the stamp's face and a 3D printer to make the handle; it can be purchased via Etsy, with profits donated to charity. In a 2019 *Washington Post* interview, Wall described his decision when selecting the stamp's portrait of Tubman: "I think it's a really beautiful image and is significant in that it is the earliest known photograph of her. It also happened that her face lined up very nicely with Andrew Jackson's features when superimposed on the bill."[33] Stamping Tubman's face onto a twenty isn't illegal and the bill can still be circulated; the denomination has not changed, the paper has not been destroyed, and the Tubman Stamp does not advertise a business. And so, on a sunny autumn afternoon, I walked a few miles from my home over to Kilgore Books with some banknotes in my wallet, ready to stamp bills and create my own Tubman twenties.

Stamping is annotation. It is a means by which someone interacts with a text and leaves a mark of agency. And stamping a $20 banknote with Harriet Tubman's portrait is also "a bit of an 'F Off,'" according to Dave (that's not his real name and that's not exactly what he said). Dave assisted me at Kilgore Books, mentioned that few people were stamping Tubman twenties at the moment, and recalled that customer participation was much higher during the Trump presidency. I asked how Kilgore became an

2.4 My first Tubman twenty created using a Tubman Stamp at Kilgore Books in Denver, Colorado. Photograph by author (2021).

official Stamping Station and he recalled visiting a comic shop in another city, marking his first bills, and then acquiring a Tubman Stamp for Kilgore. We chatted about President Jackson's role in the genocidal Trail of Tears and why people resist Tubman's placement on the twenty ("I don't get that," he said). Given that Dave sells used books and comics, I appreciated his comment that stamps are "kind of like pre-digital social media."

While visiting Kilgore, my conversation with Dave reminded me of something that Dano Wall shared in an interview with journalist Joy Reid. Wall noted: "I think we live in a racist society and currency by virtue of its ubiquity has the power to spread ideas about who we are as a nation and what we represent."[34] Similarly, historian Lusane observes that "the images on our money, like our monuments, statues, street names, and geographical place names are now all contested territory."[35] And re/marks function as an unambiguous indicator that the material and ideological features of territory—delineating our book pages, banknotes, and landmarks—are contested. The Tubman Stamp illustrates how simple everyday objects, such as currency and stamps, can be used by anyone to become an annotator who resists and reimagines symbols of power. To date, Etsy reports that the Tubman Stamp has been purchased 7,187 times. I was gifted one for Christmas.

"JOIN THE JOURNEY"

Harriet Tubman was born Araminta Ross, in Dorchester County, Maryland, around late February or early March, in 1822. On three occasions during the summer and fall of 2022, during bicentennial celebrations of Tubman's life, I traveled through Dorchester and surrounding areas along the Harriet Tubman Underground Railroad Byway. And annotations accompanied me all along the way.

The Tubman Byway is a self-guided driving tour that consists of forty-five designed sites stretching along one hundred and twenty-five miles of Maryland's Eastern Shore and another ninety-eight miles through Delaware. The byway ends in Philadelphia. It has been designated an All-American Road, the highest distinction for a scenic byway in the country.[36] The byway meanders through "a landscape that looks much like it did close to two centuries ago when Tubman was born and raised in slavery and risked her life for freedom."[37] What began, in 2000, as a state scenic byway was transformed through years of archival and community-based research: "Sites were nominated to the National Park Service's Network to Freedom Program in recognition of their authenticity. Once Underground Railroad sites were located, state and local planners connected them together . . . approximating a route that Tubman took northward to find freedom."[38] In a related 2013 development, President Obama established the 480-acre Harriet Tubman Underground Railroad National Monument in Dorchester County (a year later, congress classified this land as the Harriet Tubman Underground National Historical Park). President Obama's executive order stated: "This landscape, including the towns, roads, and paths within it, and its critical waterways, was the means for communication and the path to freedom. The Underground Railroad was everywhere within it."[39]

We can analyze the Tubman Byway as a text, for it invites the public to read backcountry roads, navigate lesser-known histories, and "reflect on the lives of these ordinary people who did extraordinary things in pursuit of freedom."[40] Byway travelers, like me, are guided along a route that traces overlooked literacies and legacies. Historian Martha S. Jones also traveled the byway in 2022 and subsequently wrote that Tubman's "epic rescues of scores of enslaved people were possible because Tubman knew how to navigate the region's contours and trails, depths and denseness, flora and fauna, the seasons, sun and stars."[41] Furthermore, I consider the byway to be an annotated text. Most of its sites feature thoughtful land-marks, such as signs and exhibits alongside the road, which reveal to an observant reader how Tubman has been memorialized in public memory and every-day place.

As the Tubman Byway crosses from Maryland into Delaware, travel-ing east, it follows a winding two-lane highway known as Willow Grove Road. Coincidentally, my in-laws live in rural Delaware, right off Willow Grove Road and just a few miles from several sites along the byway. I have visited the area many times, yet I had never borrowed my father-in-law's pickup truck and followed Tubman's footsteps. I had yet to read this par-ticular text—this curated composition of place, primary source, and civic purpose—which makes legible "sites where she rescued others, received assistance and found safety."[42] My first two summer trips along the byway each lasted about a day.[43] I visited museums, churches, cemeteries, cab-ins, courthouses, and rural farmland. I crossed the Choptank River more times than I recall. And I photographed sites like the Bucktown Village Store, where Tubman first publicly resisted slavery as a child and received a traumatic head injury, as well as monuments like the distinctive Beacon of Hope monument honoring Tubman at the Dorchester County Court-house in Cambridge, Maryland. About a month after my initial visits, I returned and traveled the byway for two additional days to carefully docu-ment a distinctive set of historical markers that exemplify the critical and creative qualities of re/marks.

I glimpsed the three-sided obelisks from a distance, for they are colorful and quite tall. Of the thirty-six Tubman Byway sites in Maryland, twenty-four feature twenty-five triangular markers that "function as place-based interpretation, informing local residents and visitors about the sites' significance . . . provid[ing] orientation to the entire byway, connections to other sites and stories, and photos and images to help illustrate them."[44]

The markers prominently display their place-names—like Long Wharf, Malone's Church, Tuckahoe Neck Meeting House, and Stanley Institute—and a thematic title, such as "Living a Double Life," "In the Shadow of Justice," and "Dangerous Rendezvous." Each includes a few paragraphs of text explaining the site's relationship to Tubman and the Underground Railroad.[45] The markers are weathered, I found a few partially obscured by overgrowth and some are also dented because snowplows inadvertently knocked a couple down over the years.[46] Only by walking around a neighborhood did I locate the marker at Bayly House, in the High Street District down the street from the Dorchester County Courthouse, for it is neither mentioned in the byway's driving guide nor included on the map. Added in 2021, this location also features an augmented reality experience with a "reenactor depicting Lizzie Amby, who was enslaved at the Bayly house and escaped from slavery through Harriet Tubman's network."[47]

The Tubman Byway markers exhibit various images, such as photographs, primary sources, and original artwork. Seven markers incorporate paintings by the eminent artist Jacob Lawrence selected from two well-known series that he created about Tubman and Frederick Douglass. Elizabeth Catlett's famous "Harriet" linocut adorns one marker that addresses her literacies: "Tubman learned how to navigate creeks and wetlands, forests, and fields in settings similar to this. She knew where to find food and shelter, and how to move about unseen." Five markers display paintings by Mark Priest, a painter and art professor, whose vivid works represent events like Tubman's liberation of her parents in 1857. "I know that history should not be forgotten," Priest told me, for "being able to, in a small way, retrace the steps of those that walked before us, and grasp greater understanding of their journey, enhances our journey in life and broadens our understanding of the world around us."[48] And four markers also quote Tubman—at Church Creek, the New Revived United Methodist Church in Taylors Island, the Harriet Tubman Underground Railroad State Park and Visitor Center, and at Brodess Farm near her birthplace. The marker at Church Creek includes a bittersweet reflection about her journey across the Mason Dixon line: "I was free; but there was no one to welcome me to the land of freedom, I was a stranger in a strange land, and my home after all was down in an old cabin quarter, with the old folks, and my brothers and sisters. But to this solemn resolution I came; I was free, and they should be free also; I would make a home for them in the North, and the Lord helping me, I would bring them all there."

When reading Tubman's remarks, permanently anchored to her byway, I reconsidered how historical markers function as texts of public memory that can redress erasure. Professor of English April O'Brien argues that historical markers frequently oppress marginalized people and communities; these texts, she suggests, can reinforce inequality "by minimizing or ignoring the accomplishments or advances of [Black, Indigenous, and people of color] individuals, and . . . by providing an inaccurate account of the injustices that many BIPOC individuals endured."[49] Conversely, markers added to the Tubman Byway—which collage together historical artifacts, contemporary media, personal perspectives, and neglected truths—communicate a needed counternarrative to limited and imprecise memorialization. These markers simultaneously inform and transform, for they have reshaped the civic and commemorative landscape. Those who read the markers will also find that they all share a common verso: a map of the byway with the name and location of sites, the phrase "Join the Journey," and an invitation to "Trace Harriet Tubman's pursuit of equality, justice, and self-determination for all."

With the Tubman Byway as referent text, the markers make critical perspectives visible by annotating land once home to plantations and enslavement with stories of emancipation and justice. As the author Clint Smith writes in *How the Word Is Passed*, we must "learn and confront the story of slavery . . . by standing on the land where it happened—by remembering that land, by marking that land, by not allowing what happened there to be forgotten."[50] The Tubman Byway markers also illustrate a contradictory quality of public remembrance by establishing a network of notes that connect places once secret and underground with contemporary memorials rising prominently from the earth. And the markers "renarrate" public memory, given what scholars Catherine Squires and Aisha Upton argue is a need for "critical memorialization to read her legacy" that rejects the "tokenization of Tubman and erasure of Black resistance."[51] Twenty-five triangular obelisks mark the land and help expand our civic imagination by composing new narratives rooted in self-liberation and the struggle for social justice.

2.5 Four Tubman Byway markers located throughout Maryland: Brodess Farm near Tubman's birthplace, upper left; Harriet Tubman Underground Railroad State Park and Visitor Center, featuring a linocut by Elizabeth Catlett, upper right; High Street District and Bayly House in Cambridge, lower right; and Choptank Landing, featuring a painting by Mark Priest, lower left. Photographs by author (2022).

"YOUR $20 BILL IS COMING SOON!"

Site 13 along the Tubman Byway is the Harriet Tubman Underground Railroad State Park and Visitor Center. Opened in 2017, the seventeen-acre park includes a museum and library, offices, a large pavilion, a "Legacy Garden," and numerous pathways; it is located within the larger Tubman National Historical Park and abuts the Blackwater National Wildlife Refuge. And walking into the museum lobby, I was pleasantly surprised to see an annotated poster celebrating Harriet Tubman's birthday.

I approached three park rangers and inquired about the poster. I hadn't expected bright Sharpie markers and a social invitation to write alongside other visitors. They told me that people had regularly contributed comments to multiple posters during various Tubman bicentennial activities. This particular poster rested on a large wooden easel, with three colorful Sharpies, and declared "Happy 200th" in large handwritten letters. Dozens of notes covered it and, judging by the handwriting, many were written by children. There were drawings of hearts, balloons, and two cakes. While many people simply wrote "Happy Birthday," other accolades stated: "Happy birthday to the greatest woman to ever live;" "your brave deeds and courage are remembered;" "May your evenings be gentle & your mornings blossom. Peace be upon you;" and "Moved by your bravery!! I am inspired to do more." One anonymous mark-maker jotted, "your $20 bill is coming soon!" Like many collaborators before me, I also recognized Tubman's bicentennial by adding another commemorative mark to a shared text of remembrance.

The Visitor Center's small museum includes richly detailed exhibits about Harriet Tubman, the Underground Railroad, slavery and abolition, as well as commemorative art by local college students. The museum also displays its own version of an annotated Tubman twenty. The final exhibit, comprised of four floor-to-ceiling panels, describes Tubman's post–Civil War life in Auburn, her marriage to Nelson Davis, participation in women's suffrage, and philanthropy. The fourth and final panel mentions Tubman's passing, posthumous honors, and includes a hopeful—yet now inaccurate—note: "On April 20, 2016, Treasury Secretary Jacob J. Lew announced that Harriet Tubman's portrait will be featured on the new $20 banknote, the most popular currency in the world. It will be released in 2020 on the 100th anniversary of the passage of the 19th Amendment,

2.6 A bicentennial birthday poster signed by visitors at the Harriet Tubman Underground Railroad State Park and Visitor Center. Photograph by author (2022).

2.7 A Tubman twenty created for an exhibit at the Harriet Tubman Underground Railroad State Park and Visitor Center. Photograph by author (2022).

which gave women the right to vote." Below, one of the museum's final images is cleverly crafted to extend Tubman's legacy through our present day. An annotated twenty appears on the panel. Her silhouette is added to the banknote, "Tubman" is inscribed beneath and "Coming Soon" is emblazoned at center. Park staff who curated this exhibit were opportune annotators whose civic composition presents visitors with a concluding counternarrative that invokes a more just social future.

"HER MARK"

Harriet Tubman was an annotator.

That Tubman was an annotator is not a figurative proposition, though surely historian Lusane's assertion is undeniable: "One of the individuals whose acts of resistance have permanently left her mark on the nation is Harriet Tubman."[52] Rather, we can return to Tubman's pension file, and her fight for rightful compensation, to read—in ink—how Tubman knowingly and permanently left her mark as an act of public resistance and recognition.

From 1890 through 1898, and on at least nine occasions, Harriet Tubman repeatedly remarked on her legacy, determined to be acknowledged by the US government for what she had accomplished and what she was owed. Her mark was an "X." And Tubman first added it to a Declaration for Widow's Pension form, dated July 14, 1890, and submitted to the Bureau of Pensions within a month after passage of the 1890 Pension Act. Tubman was sixty-eight when she wrote that X. She also added her mark to five General Affidavit forms—on August 13, 1891; February 1, 1892; November 28, 1892; June 16, 1894; and May 7, 1895—in which she testified about her husband Nelson Davis' military service, the value of her home, personal assets and debts, her prior marriage to John Tubman, as well as the veracity of statements transcribed by her pension attorney. She also marked two additional depositions, handwritten by her attorney on May 28, 1892, and November 10, 1894, regarding Nelson Davis' alias as Nelson Charles.[53] And there is, lastly, the 1898 claim against the government for $1,800. On each of these documents, her attorney wrote "Harriet Davis"—one notes "Harriet Davis late Harriet Tubman"—and the phrase "Her Mark" to represent the affiant's signature. And then, onto each, Tubman added her mark.

Once I noticed Tubman's X throughout her pension file, what could be interpreted as nine unsophisticated marks became a small corpus of

2.8 Harriet Tubman's handwritten "X" mark added to four documents to support her claim for a pension: Declaration For Widow's Pension form, July 14, 1890, top (Tubman Pension File, 26); affidavit of deposition by Tubman, August 13, 1891, middle top (Tubman Pension File, 60); affidavit of deposition by Tubman, May 28, 1892, middle bottom (Tubman Pension File, 4); claim submitted to US Congress, 1898, bottom. National Archives.

wonder and admiration. Her X always appears between "Harriet" and "Davis," as well as beneath "her" and above "mark," confirming her centered attestation and, perhaps, also suggesting that attorney McCarty wrote after Tubman's annotation. The thickness of ink also varies, both among her marks and sometimes between the two lines of an individual X. In a few instances, "her mark" has shifted orientation, presenting in appearance as similar to that of a + sign. Throughout most of the 1800s, people wrote using pens with metal nibs, dipping the pen into an inkwell and then carefully making marks on paper. As did Harriet Tubman.

Just as Tubman's 1899 Widow's Pension form was annotated and yet overlooked by prior scholarship, so, too, were the nine X inscriptions as indisputable evidence of her literacy. She was not, as many have suggested, illiterate. As we have read, she had great literacy of place, people, and mobility that nurtured her perseverance. Recently, historian Tiya Miles echoed this sentiment when writing about Tubman's "pronounced ecological consciousness" which was "required to survive enslavement and mastermind escapes across 'wild' spaces."[54] On paper, Tubman's marks were a social accomplishment, for every document that features her X also includes two signatures by witnesses who joined in her truth-telling and advocacy (some of these affidavits included the parenthetical and patronizing instruction, "If affiant signs by mark two persons who write sign here"). Tubman's acts as an annotator were expressly critical, for her marks deliberately resisted the government's disregard of her military service as she demanded a justified and secure monthly income. Her marks also evidence relentless intellectualism, for having successfully navigated treacherous land on journeys of emancipation, surely she would chart her renumeration through the procedural morass of the Bureau of Pensions. And Tubman's marks were civic actions, written so that the constraints of bureaucracy were bent closer toward the ideals of democracy. Her marks—which she traced again and again for nearly a decade and which we should see and celebrate—were a public composition authored to contest personal and systemic injustice.

Re/marks have long augmented Harriet Tubman's life and recursively rewritten her legacy. Today, Tubman's public memory continues to be composed thanks, in part, to justice-aligned acts of annotation.

3

MARKING BOUNDARIES

We are annotators who can line marges of paper and place.

During the summer of 2019, at La Casa del Túnel—an arts center located in Tijuana, but a few feet from America's fortified border wall—a group of "*rascuache* artists" traced with their hands large-scale portraits of migrants who had entered the United States as children.[1] Over nine days, the artists traced and painted seven grayscale portraits, which were then cut into strips and added to slats along the barrier stretching from sandy beach into the Pacific Ocean. The Playas de Tijuana Mural Project was "installed on the fragmented bars that make up the fence," as "a community mural that aims to bring to public attention the United States childhood arrivals dilemma."[2] In 2021, eight more portraits were added to further "communicate the unethical deportation practices."[3] When I visited, two years later, the mural was disintegrating as water and wind facilitated a gradual erasure. Someone had placed atop the rusted wall a framed portrait of Our Lady of Guadalupe. Faded and affixed beneath razor wire, her patroness watched over the weathered faces of Isaac Rivera, John Guzman, Jose, Jose Avila Flores, Chris Cuauhtli, Alex Murillo, Daniel Ruiz, Juana Mendez, Robert Vivar, Javier Salazar, Karla Estrada, Monserrat Godoy, Andy De Leon, Tania Mendoza, and Jairo Lozano.

During the winter of 1848, in Mexico City—near the town of Guadalupe Hidalgo, where the Treaty of Peace, Friendship, Limits, and Settlement was signed on February 2 of that year—a group of American diplomats and military officers also made a tracing intended for the public. It was a hand-drawn map delimiting the boundary along land that, today, includes Playas de Tijuana. While negotiating an end to the Mexican–American War,[4] a US Army captain either copied or directed the tracing of Plano del Puerto de San Diego, a map in an 1802 Spanish atlas that was an updated version of sailor Don Juan Pantoja y Arriaga's 1782 original. The traced map was both additive and reductive; it was marked with new notes and it also excised multiple details. One annotation was a ruled straight line labeled, in cursive: "Boundary Line Linea Divisoria." The map, once signed and sealed, became the authenticated treaty copy of the Plan of the Port of San Diego that is mentioned in Article V of the Treaty of Guadalupe Hidalgo. A marked map delineated the US–Mexico border.

There are powerful re/marks connecting an annotated 1848 treaty map with a twenty-first-century mural designed "to reclaim the border wall and plaster [migrants'] stories onto it."[5] Today, murals, mariposa, graffiti, hashtags, and names mark the wall; American fencing and wall infrastructure have marked the border since the 1940s; before these barriers were built, the boundary was marked with stone monuments; and the international boundary was first drawn as a line, added atop a traced map, that was attached to the text of a treaty. In this chapter, we will retrace how annotators—including artists and engineers, bureaucrats and military veterans—have written, read, and resisted this border by marking the boundary.

"AN UNNATURAL BOUNDARY"

The US–Mexico border stretches for almost two thousand miles and eschews reduction. The border line bisects cultures and ecologies, crosses water and land, and is a paradox of separation and connection; it is "both open and closed; both ordinary and traumatic."[6] Movement and constraint commingle—people and animals migrate, infrastructure develops and divides, indigenous sovereignty of the O'odham is restricted as capital flows, social policies and political agendas shift, and families are displaced and reunited. Given our attention to hybrid expression—and the divergent qualities of re/marks that both inscribe injustice and inspire social

3.1 The Playas de Tijuana Mural Project and a portrait of Our Lady of Guadalupe marking the US–Mexico border wall. Photograph by author (2023).

change—it's appropriate that I foreground how scholar and poet Gloria Anzaldúa discerned borderland dualities and incongruities: "A border is a dividing line, a narrow strip along a steep edge. A borderland is a vague and undetermined place created by the emotional residue of an unnatural boundary. It is in a constant state of transition. The prohibited and forbidden are its inhabitants."[7] The border is neither monolithic nor homogenous and the line remains both authoritative and artificial. This unnatural boundary's truths and transgressions are myriad and also include this fact: The US–Mexico border is an annotation.

The international boundary between Mexico and the US was drawn by hand as a line on a map—it was the addition of a note to a text. What, today, seems fixed and conspicuous appeared in 1848 as an annotation marked by "diplomats who, lacking accurate geographic knowledge of the territory through which a boundary was to run, ruled a line upon a map."[8] The subsequent traces of this annotation—from monuments of stone piles and concrete obelisks "erected on the line" in the late 1840s,[9] to the relatively recent addition of fences and walls[10]—are material manifestations of handwritten notes. The border is as much a social and political construct as it is "a literal construction site."[11] And parts of this construction include annotation. As historian Katherine Morrissey observes, "marking and defining the U.S.-Mexico border has been an ongoing process, involving diplomatic negotiations, mapmaking, national policies, and international agreements, along with tangible markers on the landscape: monuments, fences, and walls."[12] These tangible landmarks are also annotated with words and images. Annotators, as we will see, have put their bodies on the line to defy indignities and honor perseverance.

My decision to present the US–Mexico international boundary as an annotation is not intended to elide borderlands complexities given generational displacement, geopolitical instability, and America's legacy of racialized and inhumane migration policy.[13] Nor do I suggest this material and ideological construction be reduced for convenient interpretation. Rather, one irrefutable detail amidst long-term dilemma and crisis is the fact that the border is a literal annotation. And how might we read this line and its many re/marks? Transborder scholar Norma Iglesias Prieto explains: "From the Mexican side of the border, the wall reads like the material and social expression of the geopolitical demarcation, like the most dense and meaningful object that condenses (or contains) all the power asymmetry between Mexico and the United States. From the Mexican side of the border, we are not able to dissociate object from concept."[14] Annotation, as I will illustrate, makes object–concept associations visible and actionable, as this literacy practice usefully describes nearly two centuries of annotator mark-making that has created, demarcated, and contested this boundary.

In this chapter, we will read about a particular place of recursive boundary marking: "The limit separating Upper from Lower California," such as it was referred to in Article V of the Treaty of Guadalupe Hidalgo. Today, this limit is the boundary between San Diego and Tijuana. Why this location? Of the two maps added to the treaty's text, only the Plan of the Port of San Diego was traced from another map and annotated with the boundary line.[15] Following the treaty's ratification, it was from this point on the Pacific coast where both countries commenced to survey the border line; the Mexican Boundary Commission and the first of four US Boundary Commissions met together in San Diego in early July of 1849.[16] Another reason to concentrate our attention on this place concerns prominence. Today, while few people from either nation have crossed the line, the San Diego–Tijuana region has witnessed—compared with all other areas of this border over the past decade—the greatest number of people crossing the boundary.[17] And finally, of the many ways to describe this location and its marks—Playas de Tijuana, the limit, la frontera, a point on the Pacific Ocean, or Friendship Park—it is also a *marge*. "Like the margin between the end of type on this page and the edge of the page itself," writes landscape historian John Stilgoe, "every beach is marginal, literally the marge, a limicole zone contested by wilderness and human order."[18] For generations, the San Diego–Tijuana marge has been contested by a legacy of land-marks and re/marks added to the boundary.

I walked along this unnatural boundary in March of 2023, five months before US Customs and Border Protection began installing a new thirty-foot-high wall.[19] Consequently, much of the art and annotation that I documented was removed, including my contribution to the barrier (figure 3.2). "As the wall comes down," the *San Diego Union-Tribune* reported that summer when construction commenced, "so do the colorful murals on the Mexican side that artists have used to express thoughts on U.S.-Mexico immigration policy and migration."[20] Had I visited Playas de Tijuana during this latest phase of fortification, I would have also seen a twelve-foot-tall slab of the Berlin Wall donated to the city of Tijuana, dedicated that August and now permanently displayed but a few yards from the border barrier.[21] A small plaque affixed to the base of this three-ton concrete fragment—and which I would have read as a re/mark—is titled "Un Mundo Sin Muros" and includes this message: "Que sea esto una enseñanza para construir una sociedad que derribe muros y construye puentes de solidaridad y entendimiento, buscando siempre el bien común, la justicia social, la libertad y el hermanamiento."[22]

As you read this chapter, notice how annotators enact multiple literacy practices when marking this marge. We will see critical expression, with power (re)inscribed across the border's natural and built environment. Annotations will distill, and synthesize, opposing perspectives to reveal the boundary as both enduring scar and malleable palimpsest. And our attention to civic action will highlight the public composition of justice-directed narratives across the line.

3.2 I added Gloria Anzaldúa's phrase to the wall along the US–Mexico boundary at Playas de Tijuana (this wall section was subsequently removed). Photograph by author (2023).

"A COPY IS HEREUNTO ADDED"

The two-year Mexican–American War ended in early February, 1848, when four annotators added their signatures and stamped seals to the Treaty of Guadalupe Hidalgo: José Bernardo Couto, Miguel de Atristain, Luis Gonzaga Cuevas, and Nicholas Trist. Trist was the American diplomat who led negotiations with the Mexican government. The previous October, President Polk had recalled Trist as his efforts during armistice were regarded as unproductive.[23] Trist, however, defied the president, continued to negotiate peace terms, and was the only American to sign the treaty. Mexico agreed to cede 55 percent of its territory to the US, including land that today includes California, Nevada, Utah, and New Mexico, most of Arizona and Colorado, as well as parts of Oklahoma, Kansas, and Wyoming. Article V of the treaty delimited "the boundary line between the two Republics," and stipulated, in part:

And, in order to preclude all difficulty in tracing upon the ground the limit separating Upper from Lower California, it is agreed that the said limit shall consist of a straight line drawn from the middle of the Rio Gila, where it unites with the Colorado, to a point on the coast of the Pacific Ocean, distant one marine league due south of the southernmost point of the port of San Diego, according to the plan of said port made in the year 1782 by Don Juan Pantoja, second sailing-master of the Spanish fleet, and published at Madrid in the year 1802, in the atlas to the voyage of the schooners Sutil and Mexicana; of which plan a copy is hereunto added, signed and sealed by the respective Plenipotentiaries.

The foundational artifact that grounds our reading of borderland re/marks is the authenticated treaty copy of the Plan of the Port of San Diego described in Article V.[24] During negotiations, Mexican and American commissioners vehemently disagreed about whether the boundary line would run along the thirty-second parallel of latitude.[25] Was San Diego located in Alta California—and thus within US territory—or would it remain in Baja California as part of Mexico?[26] Both delegations proposed various boundary limits, debated geographical facts, and marshalled evidence from maps and records to contest San Diego's location. Ninety years after the negotiations, a US Department of State report found that "the material before Trist which was relevant to the question of the historic line between the two Californias was incomplete and in part erroneous; and Trist's reasoning therefrom was biased."[27] Nonetheless, when the boundary was delimited "distant one marine league due south of the southernmost point of the port of San Diego," both nations agreed that the line be ruled in reference to a 1782 map.

The brevity with which Article V mentions this map and its maker obscures a far more complex provenance. In 1782, Don Juan Pantoja—pilot of the vessel *La Princesa*, charged with supplying Spanish missions in California—drew the map Plano del Puerto de San Diego Situado en la Costa Septentrional de la California.[28] He revised his map in 1786.[29] Between 1789 and 1844, versions were reproduced in English, French, Spanish, and Mexican atlases.[30] An 1802 atlas, published in Madrid by Josef Espinosa y Tello, featured Pantoja's map as item No. 5.[31] This atlas supplemented Tello's written account of the 1792 Pacific coast voyage of the *Sutil* and the *Mexicana*;[32] that expedition did not include Pantoja, yet those are the "schooners" mentioned in Article V when citing his map. Pantoja's 1782 map, a beautiful pen-and-ink and watercolor composition, is held at the Library of Congress Geography and Map Division. During my visit, I compared Tello's plan No. 5 with the original. Tello's version features labeled place names in lieu of Pantoja's lettered legend. The reproduction also updated latitude and longitude measures, organized two explanatory notes about the bay's tides and soundings, and was signed by two engravers who drew the maps for Tello's atlas—"Cardano lo grabó," and "Morata lo escribió."

Tello's atlas was among many references that American officials consulted during treaty negotiations with Mexico. And a US Army captain, or a cartographer that he supervised, created a new tracing of Pantoja's map from the atlas. Notably, this 1848 tracing of an 1802 version of the 1782 original was not a precise duplication. The traced map's scale was moved. The two notes were removed, as were all marks indicating tides and soundings, and the names of engravers Cardano and Morata. Further, as historian Paula Rebert recalls, "no designations of latitude or longitude were given anywhere on the tracings of Pantoja's plan, so that the boundary between the Californias was delimited in relationship to the topography, the features of the land surface."[33] We recognize this altered tracing—what is called "a copy," despite not being a facsimile—as an annotation, for the map was "hereunto added" and physically attached to the treaty text.

After the Plan of the Port of San Diego was traced, it was annotated and authenticated. Most of the annotations, you will observe, make the treaty's terms visible. One prominent mark is the ruled "Boundary Line Linea Divisoria"—it literally is "a straight line drawn"—bisecting land and water south of Punta de Arena. There is also handwritten text below the boundary line; English is on the left and Spanish on the right. With these notes, the plenipotentiaries attested that this was Pantoja's map referred to in Article V and concluded: "Witness our hands and seals/Y para que conste, lo firmamos y sellamos." The four plenipotentiaries signed the map and Trist's seal was stamped on the version featured as figure 3.3.[34] The lines that comprise this authenticated map—lines both traced and ignored, drawn and written—helped define and direct geopolitical relations whose social consequences extend into our present day. Moreover, even these nineteenth-century annotations were not the only notes added to a more contemporary copy of the Plan of the Port of San Diego that I also viewed at the Library of Congress.

Nearly a century after the Plan of the Port of San Diego was traced, annotated, authenticated, and attached to the treaty, officials at the Library

MARKING BOUNDARIES 53

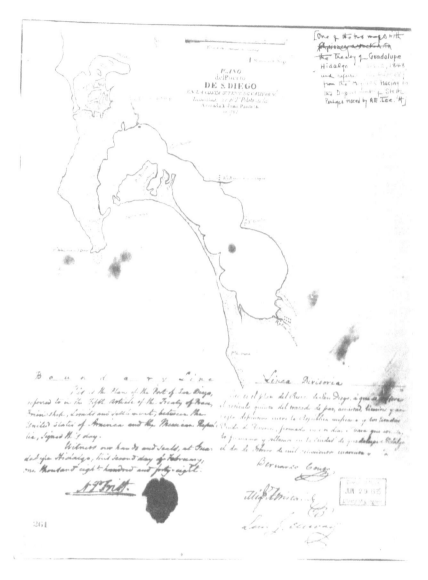

3.3 Annotated photostat of the authenticated treaty copy of the Plan of the Port of San Diego, attached to the US copy of the Treaty of Guadalupe Hidalgo, 1848. Library of Congress.

of Congress made additional annotations to a photostat of the map. Penciled in the lower left corner is "1848." A stamp marks the lower right corner: "Division of Maps Jun 29 1935 Library of Congress." A bracketed note, located in the upper right corner, was likely written about the same time as the stamp. It reads: "One of the two maps with the Treaty of Guadalupe Hidalgo on Feb. 2, 1848, and referred to in Article V; from the original tracing in the Department of State. Perhaps traced by R.E. Lee." This annotation is also emended, for the second line is struck-through. Distinctive "LM" initials accompany the note. I confirmed with Carissa Pastuch, a reference librarian with the Geography and Map Division, that annotator "LM" was Colonel Lawrence Martin. Martin was an esteemed geographer who served as chief of the division from 1924 until 1946.[35] In 1937, he wrote a short essay about the purpose and provenance of the Plan of the Port of San Diego. Martin's map annotation was echoed in his published commentary: "It seems that Captain Robert E. Lee, U.S.A., either made or directed the making of the tracing of 1848."[36]

Did Robert E. Lee trace the Plan of the Port of San Diego? The copyist didn't sign the traced map despite removing the names of engravers Cardano and Morata. It is well established, however, that Lee was a skilled cartographer. During the Mexican–American War, he was, in his own words, "taken up entirely in Constructing Maps of the Roads to Cumanaca, Toluca, Morelia, Guadalajara . . . and the mining Regions in their Vicinity."[37] Lee directly assisted Trist during treaty negotiations and provided him with "a memorandum of latitudes" regarding San Diego's location no later than January 7, 1848.[38] And on January 15, Lee wrote to Trist: "Sir, I return the volume from which the map was copied I handed you some days since."[39] When he returned "the volume"—what we know was Tello's atlas—Lee confirmed he previously and personally handed Trist the copied map. As Martin concluded, "the time when it was agreed between Trist and the Mexican Commissioners that an authenticated copy of the map of Pantoja should be added to the treaty was between January 9 and 15, 1848."[40] Whether or not Lee was the copyist, I consider him an annotator.

Why? At the very least, Lee directed a modified tracing from an atlas that he borrowed, creating a "copy" of Pantoja's map marked with a new boundary line, which he then delivered to Trist knowing that the map would be authenticated and added to the Treaty of Guadalupe Hidalgo.

Historian Rachel St. John assesses the meaning of this moment amidst the treaty's final terms, observing that the "process of delimiting, or drawing, the boundary line on paper, simple as it may seem, was the culmination of decades of conflict and diplomatic negotiation. The territorial limits . . . were laden with national significance, symbolizing a great national triumph for the United States and an even greater loss for Mexico."[41] While Lee is often associated with another boundary—the Mason–Dixon line—he also operated among a group of powerful American annotators whose collective legacy includes handmade marks of conquest and division.

"MARKED ON THE GROUND"

Mexican and American boundary marking continued throughout the second half of the nineteenth century as lines ruled by men atop maps were marked with built monuments on land. The Treaty of Guadalupe Hidalgo, ratified during the spring of 1848, required that "the two Governments shall each appoint a commissioner and a surveyor, who, before the expiration of one year from the date of the exchange of ratifications of this treaty, shall meet at the port of San Diego, and proceed to run and mark the said boundary in its whole course." Yet, as we read, the treaty delimited a boundary based upon inaccurate and insufficient geographic knowledge of the actual territory. This inevitably resulted in difficulty "running the line" across the borderland.[42] For instance, in his 1850 report, José Salazar Ylarregui—surveyor of the first Mexican Boundary Commission—emphasized the inherent difference between marking papel and el terreno: "En el papel se tira fácilmente una línea con una regla y un lápiz; pero en el terreno no es lo mismo."[43]

Today, we can more easily follow—thanks to surveyors' documentation and contemporary scholarship—marks made along the line during the binational boundary surveys, the first of which occurred between 1849 and 1856. At the time, however, numerous difficulties and discrepancies arose while marking the line. For example, a "clarification," known as the Gadsden Treaty in the US and the Mesilla Treaty in Mexico, was needed to "fix" the line, with America purchasing from Mexico thirty thousand square miles of land south of the Gila River in 1853.[44] Decades later, a second survey and "re-marking" of the boundary by the International

Boundary Commission (IBC; today, the International Boundary and Water Commission), from 1891 to 1896, further ensured that "under the treaties of 1848 and 1853 the boundary was marked by monuments of stone and iron."[45] Thus, over a fifty-year period—and despite political instability in both countries, the commissions' bureaucratic and scientific challenges, environmental changes like shifting riverbeds, and revisions to maps and treaties—boundary surveyors re-marked the land and made the line visible. These annotators facilitated an additive and iterative process of largescale land-marking that underscores historian Rebert's conclusion that the "true boundary was the boundary marked on the ground."[46]

One distinctive land-mark is Monument No. 258 located on the Pacific marge. The form of this trace has changed noticeably over time. It began as rocks piled together on October 10, 1849. The rocks were replaced by Monument No. 1, a sixteen-foot-tall white marble obelisk, erected in June of 1851. In 1894, it was repaired, enclosed by a spiked fence, and renamed as No. 258. Currently, the marker is wedged alongside America's border wall. And, as I learned, it's only accessible from Playas de Tijuana.

The US–Mexico border is marked by 276 monuments.[47] This corpus, in our terms, comprises the first material traces made on the borderlands as an annotated environment. Fifty-two monuments were originally added on the line by the first boundary survey and, as environmental historian C. J. Alvarez assesses, "the initial border markers did a terrible job of marking the border."[48] Some were constructed of cast iron or cut stone—of these, fourteen were inscribed—though "the majority were but rude piles of stone."[49] The distance between monuments varied from one-eighth of a mile to over eighty. Predictably, some were inaccurately "footed" on the line and others were destroyed or dismantled by locals seeking building materials.[50] In the early 1890s, American officials referred to the original markers as the "old" monuments and tersely summarized the state of prior boundary marking: "The boundary, originally marked with an inadequate number of monuments, many of them unsubstantial and without distinctive features, had become almost obliterated." Four decades after the boundary was marked, sixteen monuments were found to be "tumbling to pieces." Nine were described as "no trace remaining;" among these, two were "probably never erected." Two more were "entirely demolished."

MARKING BOUNDARIES 57

OLD MONUMENT NO. 1, ON THE PACIFIC.   ANTIGUO MONUMENTO NO. 1, EN EL PACÍFICO.

3.4 Old Monument No. 1, On The Pacific, prior to repair, 1894. International Boundary Commission, Report of the Boundary Commission Upon the Survey and Re-Marking of the Boundary Between the United States and Mexico West of the Rio Grande, 1891 to 1896: Parts 1 and 2. University of North Texas Libraries.

3.5 Monumento Número 258, after remodel, 1894. International Boundary Commission, *Vistas De Los Monumentos Á Lo Largo De La Línea Divisoria Entre Mexico y Los Estados Unidos De El Paso Al Pacifico*. Texas Tech University.

And given its prominence, Old Monument No. 1 was "badly defaced by visitors" and "so mutilated . . . that its outlines were nearly destroyed and its inscriptions partly obliterated."[51] Forty-three of the original markers would be repaired or replaced. Like book marginalia that fades or is erased, the old monuments weathered and some disappeared; and just as annotators rewrite lines, the border was re-marked.

Two hundred and fifteen obelisks were added to the border during the second boundary survey by the IBC. This survey was a more "modernist" effort of scientific and technological ingenuity, writes historian Morrissey, "to create permanent meanings and scientific lines."[52] The new markers measured over six-feet tall, weighed more than seven hundred pounds, and were cast of prefabricated iron. These standardized monuments were conspicuously footed no more than a few miles apart. The second survey also (re)numbered and inscribed all the markers, from east to west, starting with the new Monument No. 1 on the bank of the Rio Grande and continuing to Monument No. 258 on the Pacific. Erecting the new monuments required sophisticated coordination among teams of engineers, astronomers, blacksmiths, stone masons, laborers, cavalry, couriers, photographers, military escorts, rodmen, levelmen, cooks, pack animals, baggage wagons, and all manner of scientific instruments, maps, weapons, construction materials, and tools. Though arduous and expensive, this land-marking represented, as Alvarez suggests, "the perpetuity of the nation-state itself."[53] In his analysis, re-marking the boundary "inaugurated the tradition of technological precision that would undergird all future border construction projects. The monuments were emblematic of this."[54] Following Alvarez, I suggest that we reappraise the mass production of boundary monuments as a project of nationalist annotation; re/marks made it easier to read the border and comprehend how a marked line separated the privileged from those perceived as foreign and inferior.

In June of 1894, when Monument No. 258 was "entirely remodeled" at a marble yard in San Diego, this marker was reinscribed with various annotations.[55] The legacy of border marking was carved into each face of the four-sided obelisk: "Boundary of the United States" appears on the north and "Limite de la Republica Mexicana" on the south; recognition of the monument's 1894 reconstruction by the IBC was added on the east; and the west face notes that this is the "Initial point of boundary/Punto inicial del Limite," as established by the Treaty of Guadalupe Hidalgo on February 2, 1848. Two documents—written in English and Spanish, each naming the commissioners and engineers who marked the line—were also deposited within a copper tube "and embedded in the foundation" beneath the remodeled monument.[56] We may perceive those notes as the monument's subterranean re/marks, concealed from view and the possibility of subversive resistance. When I visited Playas de Tijuana and read Monument No. 258, shadowed by the gaze of American surveillance infrastructure, I began to better comprehend scholar Iglesias Prieto's commentary about this boundary's layered legacy: "It went from being an imaginary line marked with some scattered monuments to a light barbed fence, to a wire grid, to a heavy metal wall, until becoming what it is today: a series of aggressive metal fences and enormous concrete posts. It stopped being more of a symbolic marker, which announced the geopolitical boundaries between two nation-states, and became and was naturalized as the major material impediment that inhibits human movement."[57]

3.6 Monument No. 258 under the gaze of American surveillance infrastructure, next to a cross added to the border wall at Playas de Tijuana (this wall section was subsequently removed). Photograph by author (2023).

"YOU NEVER SEE THE SAME MURAL AGAIN"

Lizbeth De La Cruz Santana read a handwritten annotation in the summer of 2017 that marked the border wall at Playas de Tijuana. The note addressed inhibited human movement. Yet De La Cruz Santana was initially confused and it piqued her curiosity. Ultimately, this mark informed how she guided a communal remarking of the boundary line at a "symbolic location [that] interpolates outsiders to engage the mural both as a memorial and as a critique."[58] Today, De La Cruz Santana is a professor of Chicano/a/x Studies; since 2019, she has also directed the Playas de Tijuana Mural Project and, in that role, we can admire her acts as an annotator. When I spoke with her, she mentioned how encountering border "messages" influenced the composition of a mural that extends contemporary re/marks:

I was just taking photos of the border. And I found two messages. One of them was "let us cross," and the other one was "ten years." And I was like, "Why the ten years?" I get the first one; "let us cross" could be applied to different communities. But the "ten years," for me was, "What is this? Why is that so important?" And then, when I met people who have faced deportation and actually had a ten-year bar, that's when I realized, "Oh, that's what it means."[59] What was missing at the border, at Friendship Park, with the murals and paintings . . . if you as an audience come in, maybe not really knowing anything about immigration, deportation, or why people want to migrate into the US, then that message gets lost. I felt like I needed someone, like at a museum for example, guiding you and telling you, "Oh, this is here because this is the history." When I did the mural project for the Playas de Tijuana, that was a key thing for me. I need to guide people to understand why these faces are painted. And have them tell their stories.

This community mural—which defies the criminalization of childhood arrivals in the US—was among three that marked the border wall when I visited Playas de Tijuana. It was an early Tuesday morning. A woman jogged along the beach. Children scampered among parents, while tourists strolled the Malecón with coffee snapping selfies. Cameras high atop an American tower surveilled our movements. Military helicopters circled overhead; the whir omnipresent. And so, too, was the wall. It's impossible to ignore, the metal barricade was nearly twenty-feet high at the time, an exclamation mark of authority and partition.[60]

As an annotator, I was keen to read and mark a geopolitical margin exhibiting both critical and creative re/marks. The social and aesthetic features of Playas de Tijuana recognize hope amid separation, as color brightened textured rust. Surfaces of this built environment—the sidewalks, benches, tables, sculptures, and most visibly the wall—have all been turned into texts recurrently re-marked in a polyvocal and multimodal dialogue. A large "Tijuana" sculpture stands at the promenade edge, the seven block letters each a different bold color, placed atop a pedestal that acknowledges belonging and division: "Aqui Empieza La Patria." Nearby this statue is Monument No. 258, abutting the wall. And like the barriers of other contested boundaries, from Belfast to Gaza, this wall-as-canvas was annotated with handwritten hashtags, names, dates, handprints, crosses, and memorials. The traces of this landscape concentrate contradiction, as messages, responses, and interpretation converge: "Libertad," "Free Migration For All," "Que todo lo bueno te siga, te encuentre y se quede contino," "Let Us See Each Other," "Me Espia El Et," "НЕТ ВОЙНЕ." In *Borderwall as Architecture: A Manifesto for the U.S.-Mexico Boundary*, architect Ronald Rael states: "The U.S.-Mexico wall has created a territory of paradox, horror, transformation, and flux, like the Berlin Wall did, but on a much larger scale."[61] The wall at Playas de Tijuana had been transformed by annotators critically marking the international boundary, contesting an ideology of fear, and creatively envisioning social justice. This margin fluctuates, as marks and murals are revised and recontextualized; as De La Cruz Santana told me, "you never see the same mural again."

Rael's *Manifesto* judges the border wall as "a horrifically beautiful and widely photographed land installation," that functions as "the world's largest gallery wall, enticing artists to find representation somewhere along the hundreds of miles available to them."[62] Like De La Cruz Santana, I saw how the wall enticed artist Enrique Chiu, who began painting Mural de la Hermandad on Election Day in 2016.[63] Four thousand volunteers have helped paint multiple sections of the mural, in Tijuana and elsewhere, with heartfelt messages, mariposa (a symbol of migration), and hashtags like #UnMundoSinMuros. The mural's words and images interrupt what Chiu calls "a wall of incomprehension" by creating "a final glimpse of hope for migrants risking danger as they cross northward."[64] Mural de la Hermandad is a critical—and hopeful—rejoinder to America's "build the wall" xenophobia. It also makes a counternarrative easily comprehensible: The

3.7 Mural de la Hermandad at Playas de Tijuana: Detail of painted gate featuring the phrase "Un Mundo Sin Muros," top; a section of the mural as the wall is refortified, bottom (both wall sections were subsequently removed). Photographs by author (2023).

surface and symbolism of this constructed barrier will be restoried as new marks make everyday resistance visible and suggest alternative sociopolitical possibilities. Though much of Mural de la Hermandad at Playas de Tijuana was destroyed throughout the latter half of 2023, Chiu revived communal painting as soon as the new wall was installed, stating: "Sabemos que todo arte puede ser una protesta, pero queremos hacerlo de manera pacífica como siempre lo hemos hecho y dejar un mensaje positivo a la comunidad migrante, de Tijuana y del otro lado de la frontera."[65]

Given its scale, the version of Mural de la Hermandad that I experienced surrounded another mural created, in 2013, by artist and US Navy veteran Amos Gregory. Gregory initially collaborated with a group of about twenty American military veterans to paint the Deported Veterans Mural Project on the wall; today, the number of contributing veterans has tripled.[66] The mural has shifting features, for it utilizes the wall's slats to reveal multiple images when viewed from different angles. Looking northeast, I read "Repatriate" in large red letters, next to an upside-down American flag—traditionally interpreted as a military distress signal—with fifty inverted crosses replacing the flag's stars. Looking northwest, I read the many names of deported veterans painted in red and blue; most veterans' names were paired with an abbreviation of their military branch, and a few were followed by "RIP." A slat noted: "In honor of all the U.S. vets who have been deported. Bring them home now." By one estimate, at least one thousand veterans have been deported from the US and now live in approximately forty countries.[67] Reading the mural, my awareness of contradictory re/marks made visible a bitter truth: Over 175 years ago, men in the American military ruled a line atop an altered map that became a boundary now marked by a wall which displayed the painted names of deported veterans who recently served the same country. The mural was a testament to collective service and individual sacrifice while also indicting systemic indignity. In early 2024, the Deported Veterans Mural Project was destroyed during barrier reconstruction. A section of the mural was saved by a local community coalition and may be displayed in the future.[68]

Some veterans painted their own names on the wall when contributing to the Deported Veterans Mural Project. That was the case for Alex Murillo, who grew up in Phoenix, served in the US Navy, and was deported to Mexico in 2011. Thanks to new policies, the father of four returned home

MARKING BOUNDARIES

3.8 Photographing the Deported Veterans Mural Project with Alex Murillo's name in the foreground, 2023 (this wall section was subsequently removed). Courtesy of Francisco Perez.

in 2022.[69] Murillo is also an annotator "who worked on the mural and wrote his name on it."[70] And, distinctively, Murillo's annotations appeared repeatedly on this margin; a few years after he added his name to the wall, Murillo connected with De La Cruz Santana to trace and install his portrait further down the line as part of the Playas de Tijuana Mural Project.

"TO LEAVE A MARK FOR THEM"

De La Cruz Santana read the "ten years" re/mark while conducting fieldwork with Humanizing Deportation, a multi-institutional storytelling project whose archive includes hundreds of digital narratives addressing the consequences of border control and immigration policy.[71] After encountering the annotation, she wondered: "How do I get other people

3.9 Painting the Playas de Tijuana Mural Project portrait of Jose, summer of 2021. Courtesy of Lizbeth De La Cruz Santana.

3.10 Installing the Playas de Tijuana Mural Project on the border wall, summer of 2021. Courtesy of Lizbeth De La Cruz Santana.

to understand the things that I am currently learning?" Supported by fellowships and funding, De La Cruz Santana partnered with artists Mauro Carrera and Enrique Chiu, collaborated with people whose stories were featured in Humanizing Deportation (including veteran Alex Murillo), and organized the resources and volunteers needed to install the Playas de Tijuana Mural Project on the wall. The storytellers-turned-muralists were not trained artists, yet "we became artists through the process." And that participatory process included tracing photographs onto cloth: "We used a projector to project the images onto the material that we used and then we outlined their faces with Sharpies or pencils and painted them."[72] On the beach, during the summers of 2019 and 2021, the wall was cleaned, then primed and painted, before each portrait's eight cloth strips were glued to slats. Given the heat and waves, marking the boundary with the mural was "extremely dangerous," De La Cruz Santana recalled, "but we did it."

The Playas de Tijuana Mural Project marks the boundary with fifteen faces and stories. De La Cruz Santana made the mural's narrative feature widely accessible by adding another type of note to the wall—interactive QR codes. These annotations are material additions to the border wall and an attribute of the mural's composition that serves multiple purposes. First, portrait-specific QR codes link to corresponding digital stories in Humanizing Deportation's archive—visitors to each portrait can scan a code and watch the storyteller's video. Second, the codes guide interpretation, helping viewers to better understand the "real face behind people that are often criminalized, as people don't really understand why someone can get deported." Third, each code is a digital trace encouraging social interaction: "After listening to the story, [visitors] can then make a choice to share it with their networks."[73] And fourth, while QR codes mark the built environment—and, in Tijuana, are another expression of boundary marking—this form of annotation easily transcends physical barriers, and political borders, to inform social discourses. QR codes are among the many reasons why the Playas de Tijuana Mural Project is more than a local landmark: "The mural was only meant for the community that was being represented," De La Cruz Santana shared with me. "It was a way for us to bond together, to do something that was going to leave a mark for them. But it became this big thing. I didn't expect that, you know, to bloom this way."

Throughout a contested history, the US–Mexico boundary has never not been marked—especially along the San Diego–Tijuana marge—and the Playas de Tijuana Mural Project is a recent, justice-centered re/mark. Whereas the borderland's nineteenth-century markers persist as monuments of stone, mostly identical and entirely bureaucratic, separating nations, this mural's portraits appear monumental in scale, wholly unique and expressly sympathetic, connecting people. The Playas de Tijuana Mural Project is a critical marker opposing what Rael calls a "wall of death"[74] by annotating the barrier with stories of hope and home. The mural is also a marker of contrasting realities, displaying endurance amidst erasure, for "this mural is meant to fade" De La Cruz Santana emphasized. The eroding faces represent, as she writes, "a symbolic erasure and silence of the deportation of childhood arrivals in academic, political, and social movement practices."[75] And the mural is a civic statement signaling transborder possibilities. With storytellers' comments emerging from and moving over the wall, De La Cruz Santana informed me that related civic advocacy has successfully reunited families: "Alex Murillo came back. Andy De Leon came back. Robert Vivar came back. And then two of the Dreamers became permanent residents. So then what about everyone else?"

Seven months after we first spoke, I asked De La Cruz Santana about the Playas de Tijuana Mural Project given construction developments. She shared this update: "For now, it seems like the border fence reconstruction won't impact the mural. But only time will tell."[76] She is also planning to mark this ever-shifting marge with a third set of portraits and stories.

While humane border and migration policy remains unwritten, we know that ground truths and testimonials will continue to be written along this line. For as long as an unnatural boundary divides families and communities, annotators will resist legacies of separation by authoring re/marks about more just social futures.

4

MARKED MEN

We are annotators who can broadcast monumental critique and creativity.

"I threw my blood and red ink on the statue," remarked Maya Little. "In April, I did what I've been doing this past year, which is adding historical context to the white supremacist monument known as *Silent Sam*."[1] Little, at the time, was a doctoral student in history at the University of North Carolina at Chapel Hill (UNC). After the August 2017 white nationalist rally in Charlottesville, Virginia, Little organized student sit-ins and protests throughout the 2017–18 academic year to remove the campus's Confederate Monument. Intransigence by university administrators ultimately forced Little's hands; that spring, she "contextualized" Silent Sam with her blood and red ink and was arrested. In a written statement, Little described her public action as "an opportunity to teach" and noted: "It is also our duty to continue the struggle against white supremacy . . . The statue, a symbol of UNC's commitment to white supremacy, has been defaced and protested since 1968."[2] Indeed, Silent Sam was "intended to remind viewers that those students who fought for the Confederacy were heroes of the white race," writes historian Adam Domby in *The False Cause*, as "the monument was meant, at least in part, to be an enduring testament to the success of white supremacy."[3]

Little and her peers, however, were committed to another enduring testament—the struggle against white supremacy and anti-Black racism.

And that included acts that defaced the Confederate Monument and marked resistance. Art historians call this "iconoclasm from below," as such action renders "the assault visible to symbolize ongoing protest against the existing political system."[4] In her statement, Little addressed UNC's Chancellor Carol Folt directly using the rhetoric of visual mark-making: "You should see him the way that we do, at the forefront of our campus covered in our blood."[5]

From the Black Student Movement of the 1970s to the Real Silent Sam Coalition in the 2010s, Little's efforts echoed other UNC students who had gathered around the monument to demand its removal, protest racial violence, and demonstrate against injustice.[6] And, over many years, students' re/marks of dissent highlighted the figure.[7] Red paint and graffiti appeared following Dr. Martin Luther King, Jr.'s assassination. In 2011, a mock plaque was added explaining the statue's racist history. The phrase "black lives matter," as well as "KKK" and "murderer," were spray-painted in July of 2015 after nine African Americans were killed at Mother Emanuel AME Church in Charleston, South Carolina. Weeks later, the question "Who is Sandra Bland?" was written on the base,[8] as the "continued tagging of the Confederate Monument helped to sustain a conversation on the campus about the persistence of anti-Black violence in Chapel Hill during the summer months."[9] Yet whenever Silent Sam was marked, the traces were promptly erased. The July, 2015 graffiti received a whitewashing, of sorts, from the statue: "The University responded quickly to that incident, covering it up with a white cloth until it could be struck from the base."[10] All the while, Sam was anything but silent, for the landmark—located on the campus' symbolic front lawn—distilled a communal record of racism, criticism, and erasure.

When Little, as an annotator, splattered Silent Sam with her blood and ink on April 30, 2018, she was accompanied by other activists. Two students held a banner that stated "Work Order For Folt." Others chanted "No cops, no Klan, get rid of Silent Sam!" And one student read a speech that Julian Carr delivered on June 2, 1913, during the monument's dedication. Silent Sam was erected amid "monument mania" during the first two decades of the twentieth century, in an era when Confederate monument building became "inextricably intertwined with Jim Crow racial segregation, disenfranchisement, lynching, and the [United Daughters of the

Confederacy] school textbook initiative" that taught Southern children "invented history, White supremacy, and the inferiority of African Americans as a racial group."[11] The dedication attracted one thousand people and lauded the Confederacy, glorified "Anglo Saxon" superiority, and celebrated racial violence.[12] And Carr was a fitting speaker—he was a Confederate veteran, a political and philanthropic leader, and a member of the Ku Klux Klan. Yet for nearly a century, his speech at UNC was forgotten. Only in 2011 were excerpts published, including a passage in which he bragged: "I horse-whipped a negro wench until her skirts hung in shreds, because upon the streets of this quiet village she had publicly insulted and maligned a Southern lady."[13] In the student-produced documentary *Silence Sam Film*, Little summarizes UNC's history of racial injustice, concluding: "We're out here because of this legacy."[14]

The original typed copy of Carr's monument dedication speech reveals that he was an annotator, too. What do you notice? The third sentence of his prepared address reads: "The whole Southland is sanctified by the precious blood of the fallen Confederate soldier." Before his speech, Carr struck-through "fallen" and removed this descriptor of defeat. His handwritten edit added "student" above the redaction. This revision was neither subtle nor insignificant, for it directly associated university students with the Confederacy and honored those who sacrificed "precious blood" for a pro-slavery republic. Furthermore, Carr's annotation referenced the statue's inscription (another type of note added to a text), which valorized "The Sons Of The University" and declared: "Duty Is The Sublimest Word In the English Language." In *Standing Soldiers, Kneeling Slaves*, historian Kirk Savage concludes that "images of a common soldier on a pedestal"—statues like Silent Sam—were "simple forms, immediately understood," erected by those "who claimed the right to speak for the collective."[15] In 1913, Carr and other white supremacists falsely claimed a right to speak for the UNC community. For decades, Black students and their allies contested that claim. And just over one hundred years after Carr spoke on campus, Little and her peers revoiced his commentary while re-marking the monument. A few months later, on the evening of August 20, during a protest to support Little, students toppled Silent Sam. The pedestal was removed in early 2019. Today, the statue sits in storage.[16]

that fittingly express my feelings in this presence on this occasion. But you know and I know, that though I might ~~plum~~ *Speak* with the tongue of men and of angels, neither song nor story could fittingly honor this glorious event. The whole Southland is sanctified by the precious blood of the ~~soldier~~ *Student* Confederate soldier. Their sublime courage has thrown upon the sky of Dixie a picture so bright and beautiful that neither defeat, nor disaster, nor oppression, nor smoke, nor fire, nor devasta-

4.1 Annotated selection of Julian Carr's "Unveiling of Confederate Monument at University" speech, 1913. The Wilson Library, University of North Carolina at Chapel Hill (archived at https://exhibits.lib.unc.edu/items/show/5519).

4.2 Maya Little throwing her blood and red ink on the statue known as Silent Sam, 2019. Screenshot from UNC-student produced documentary *Silence Sam Film* (available at https://www.youtube.com/watch?v=o9uQKmRipQM).

REWRITING THE MEMORIAL LANDSCAPE

"What," asks poet Caroline Randall Williams, "is a monument but a standing memory?"[17] Monuments are texts of memory. Maya Little understood that and she marked Silent Sam by adding yet another public re/mark to students' decades-long fight for a more just social future. Little annotated a standing memory and accelerated the monument's fall.

In prior chapters, I detailed how people embrace annotation—as their notes mark texts, familiar objects, and everyday places—in order to compose justice-directed narratives. So, too, with Silent Sam's removal, though this chapter doesn't analyze a single statue. Rather, our focus broadens to an expansive account of annotators who march in the streets, interpret historical artifacts, and learn as students. Historian Catherine Clinton observes that "statues and memorials tell us more about those who create these commemorations than they do about those being honored."[18] As I will argue, marked monuments tell us much about how communities read the past and rewrite present values. In a 2017 discussion about Confederate monuments, historian Nell Irvin Painter emphasized the need to "broadcast the three words 'history and memory'—just to get people to understand that such concepts exist."[19] When monuments are annotated, conspicuous notes broadcast the distinction between history and memory. And that motivates me to ask: How should we understand the marking of monuments during public protest as an act of literacy? What are the limitations of notes that contextualize monuments? And how might new monuments be imagined through creative annotation? I address these three questions because of how public monuments are contested, contextualized, and envisioned.

Annotation is an everyday literacy practice that marks both documents and monuments, because of social activity, to express critical and civic messages. As we will see, annotation is a typical, visual, and participatory intervention that usefully explains how people comprehend and respond to their *memorial landscape*. Geographers define the memorial landscape as public spaces and heritage sites where monuments and other aspects of material culture are associated with collective memory.[20] The memorial landscape surrounds us all; as ignored background, ideological battleground, and also as a marked medium. And we've already surveyed this landscape in our study of annotation. "Opening Remarks" mentioned the "History Under Construction" sign at Muir Woods National Monument. In chapter 2, I described my travels along the Harriet Tubman Underground Railroad Byway where annotators with formal cultural authority marked a historic route to share narratives about enslavement and liberation. And in chapter 3, we read about how annotators wielding moral authority marked the US–Mexico border wall with murals acknowledging division and dignity. Re/marks are etched across the surfaces and symbols of our memorial landscape, reconfiguring public monuments as texts of historical memory created by those with power to communicate ideological priorities.

The American memorial landscape is disputed on the ground and debated in the media. This occurred during Black Lives Matter demonstrations throughout the 2010s after police violence against African Americans, following Charleston in 2015 and Charlottesville in 2017, and then again after the killings of Ahmaud Arbery, Breonna Taylor, and George Floyd in 2020.[21] In her role as president of the Andrew W. Mellon Foundation, Elizabeth Alexander introduced the 2021 *National Monument Audit* by writing: "We may not notice how just a few stories have been disproportionately commemorated in a country created by multitudes. We may not know which voices are missing, which contributions have been elided, or how much the monuments and memorials now standing misrepresent our collective history."[22] That audit of 48,178 records, representing every US state and territory, concluded that monuments selectively remember preferred narratives and can "erase, deny, or belittle the historical experience of those who have not had the civic power or privilege to build them. Where inequalities and injustices exist, monuments often perpetuate them."[23] Our memorial landscape isn't fixed, certain, or neutral. As we reckon with—and also resist and reimagine—how historical memory appears in public spaces, it has also become difficult to ignore the marking of monuments.

Iconoclasm is an age-old tradition. And, admittedly, not every smashed statue or toppled idol exhibits traces of annotation. Yet Confederate generals and their foot soldiers, Christopher Columbus and Junípero Serra, and many an American president have become a brotherhood of marked men because of annotators, and whether or not their bronze and stone still shape an overwhelmingly white and male memorial landscape that reflects war, celebrates conquest, and misrepresents history.[24] This chapter concerns monuments in the US located in public settings, like a park or town square or courthouse lawn.[25] In this civic context, messages communicated by monuments—symbolic messages conveyed with images and explicit messages stated with textual inscriptions—are understood to represent government speech and the government's viewpoint.[26] And, as one response to these public messages, annotators add to their surroundings: "Monuments and memorials fall in and out of public favor as opinions about the past shift. Different social groups with different or often competing political interests and historical interpretations rewrite the memorial landscape."[27] Removing a monument, like changing a place-name, doesn't erase history, for memorials frequently fabricate the past, silence the heritage of nondominant groups, and misrepresent a community's present-day values.[28] While the fate of many monuments remains unknown, re/marks can be anticipated as public annotation rewrites America's memorial landscape.

The questions that I address about annotation enabling protest, context, and imagination are informed by appraisals of monuments offered by artists and historians, authors of graffiti and government policy, and scholars studying public memory and the politics of space.[29] Discussion about monuments in scholarship and popular media often mentions people that we will recognize as annotators. One group of annotators are activists, like Little and her UNC peers, who oppose the messages of a monument. Our first concern are protestors whose public re/marks highlight object and objection, whether their traces are celebrated as justified or criticized as vandalism. Another group of annotators are supporters of monuments who concede that dated messages require additional context. Our second focus examines efforts to contextualize monuments by adding explanatory notes on new signs or plaques. The information that ultimately complements a monument, and the effective display of that context, reveals the limits of this approach to public annotation. Lastly, we will meet a class of third-grade students in New Orleans, and their teacher, who creatively reimagined their city's memorial landscape after four Confederate monuments were removed in 2017. The students' self-published book is anything but a simple class project; rather, it's a guide celebrating how children's re/marks enable critical, creative, and civic visions. Throughout this chapter, we encounter annotators comprehending monumental messages and rewriting the memorial landscape with traces added to texts of material memory.

FIGURATIVE HIGHLIGHTING

"A more than century-old statue of Christopher Columbus inside Central Park was discovered defaced on Tuesday morning," reported the *New York Times* in the fall of 2017, "its hands stained with red paint and its pedestal scrawled with graffiti including the hashtag '#somethingscoming.'"[30] Defaced. Vandalized. Graffiti, stated with pejorative intent. Assault. Legal terms of transgression commonly describe annotated monuments. Defenders of the memorial landscape may dismiss public annotation as inappropriate expression, ascribe honor to inanimate objects, and even discredit the objections of those advocating against injustice. Let us not forget President Trump who, in response to racial justice uprisings in the summer of 2020, signed an executive order "protecting public monuments, memorials, and statues from the mob's ropes and graffiti," emphasizing that "no individual or group has the right to damage, deface, or remove any monument by use of force."[31] Rather than write off these re/marks as illegitimate or irrelevant, I suggest that we reframe how monuments are marked during public protest as an act of literacy. And the familiar vocabulary of annotation helps me name this type of re/mark as "figurative highlighting."

I define figurative highlighting as the marking of a monument with paint, blood, ink, graffiti, acronyms, hashtags, phrases, insults, cloth, yarn, projections, or handmade signs. Annotators' figurative highlighting marks a figure's surfaces and discourses by making visible opposition to the ideology of stated and symbolic messages. We should expect figurative highlighting during public protest as activists inscribe critical and civic messages across the memorial landscape. For instance, art historian Erin Thompson's *Smashing Statues* details the July 2020 toppling of the Columbus statue at the Minnesota State Capitol: "Indigenous Minnesotans had protested the Columbus monument at least since the 1970s. Almost every year on Columbus Day, someone would toss a water balloon filled with red paint—or sometimes their own blood—at its face." In 2015, Thompson recalls, "a blue sticky note covered the part of the base's inscription

MARKED MEN 79

that called Columbus 'the discoverer of America,' naming him instead 'the father of violence against Native people.'"[32] Similar figurative highlighting amplified Black Lives Matter protests, as documented by historian Karen Cox in *No Common Ground*: "In the months following the Charleston massacre, as had happened to Confederate monuments in cities throughout the South, the Lee monument was targeted by protestors who painted the pedestal with the phrase 'Black Lives Matter.' In July 2017, someone splashed the statue with red paint."[33] From a legal perspective, such acts break the law. From a critical literacy stance, however, we can comprehend figurative highlighting as the marked refusal of inherited historical memory. Figurative highlighting produces civic compositions that contest commemoration and interrupt how messages of the past are broadcast in today's public spaces.

The hybrid impressions of annotation are accentuated by figurative highlighting. Bright paint and graffiti added to a bronze statue or stone pedestal creates stark visual and rhetorical juxtaposition. Dissonance between reverence and rejection becomes immediately discernable. For example, a monument in Nashville's Centennial Park was highlighted in the summer of 2019 with "They Were Racists" spray-painted in red over a plaque honoring over five hundred Confederate soldiers. The nameless statue was splattered in red paint.[34] In other instances, the incongruity of figurative highlighting is emphasized because of material added to a monument. Artist Joiri Minaya cloaked statues of Columbus and Ponce de Leon during Miami Art Week in 2019 with fabric featuring Caribbean "plants of resistance," thereby "obscuring the identity and message of the figure" and "providing counter-narratives that question 'official,' often tourist-driven monuments that tend to romanticize troubling histories."[35] A less elaborate, through similarly provocative, use of cloth materialized in March 2019 when two white hoods resembling those worn by KKK members were placed over the figures of a Confederate monument located on the North Carolina Capitol grounds.[36] The hoods were removed, as was the monument one year later.[37] And knitted kudzu has covered Confederate monuments throughout Virginia as an anonymous group of Charlottesville craftivists, known as The Kudzu Project, employ yarn bombing methods for their "guerilla knitting" installations attached to statues that "are no longer relevant to our society."[38] Figurative highlighting most likely fades, yet that is another

4.3 Knitted kudzu covering a Confederate monument at the Nelson County Courthouse in Lovingston, Virginia, 2018. Courtesy of The Kudzu Project; photo credit Tom Cogill.

important characteristic of such annotation. These traces of dissent are temporary and, like other expressions of public protest art, are "in a state of constant change, as new conversations and dialogues emerge over time."[39] Monuments will be cleaned and re/marks erased. Yet figurative highlighting endures because images of annotated monuments circulate online among social networks. The afterlife of highlighted monuments lengthens once material marks are documented as digital media, providing annotated evidence that our memorial landscape is a contradictory construction propped atop shaky fault lines.

Figurative highlighting went viral in the summer of 2020 when words and images were projected onto the Robert E. Lee Monument in Richmond, Virginia, the Confederacy's former capitol. This grand equestrian statue was erected in 1890 despite multiple disputes and towered over sixty feet as Monument Avenue's centerpiece.[40] It was removed, after protracted legal proceedings, on September 8, 2021. Lighting up the Lee Monument had precedence; following Charlottesville, amid renewed calls for its removal, a group projected "Dismantle White Supremacy" onto the plinth. In 2020, as a widespread reckoning irrevocably altered the nation's memorial

4.4 A figurative highlighting of the Robert E. Lee Monument in Richmond, Virginia, 2017. Courtesy of Backbone Campaign/Richmond DSA.

landscape, annotators continuously marked the Lee Monument's base by "covering the marble and granite with the names of victims of police violence, protest chants, calls for compassion, revolutionary symbols and anti-police slogans in dozens of colors," thereby transforming the monument into a celebrated work of protest art.[41] And, because the ongoing protests also occurred at night, two local artists highlighted the marked monument with light.

Annotators Dustin Klein and Alex Criqui used their lighting equipment to project large portraits onto the Lee Monument. George Floyd and the phrase "No Justice No Peace" appeared across the base, with "BLM" displayed on Lee's horse. There was also a colorful portrait of Breonna Taylor. And Frederick Douglass stating: "Power concedes nothing without a demand. It never did and it never will." Images of Rosa Parks and John Lewis, Angela Davis and Jacob Lawrence, and many other African American leaders, musicians, politicians, and artists graced the statue, too. As did a portrait of Harriet Tubman from the 1870s, adding yet another public

4.5 A portrait of Harriet Tubman projected onto the Robert E. Lee Monument in Richmond, Virginia, during racial justice protests, 2020. Courtesy of Alex Criqui and Dustin Klein, Reclaiming the Monument 2020; photo credit Zach Fichter.

re/mark to her legacy. Tubman's highlighted image was accompanied by a quote published in an 1856 book (coincidentally, the first sentence of her quote adorns the Brodess Farm marker, in Maryland, along the Tubman Byway).[42] And part of her quote's penultimate sentence was projected onto the marked Lee Monument: "Slavery is the next thing to hell." In an interview during the summer 2020 protests, Klein mentioned the logistical challenges and physical dangers of this public annotation, recalling: "There was about a week where the state police were showing up to clear out the park after sundown. We moved to private property and projected from an off-center angle to not be in their way. We were able to keep the projection of Harriet Tubman on during the entire process of rubber bullets and tear gas."[43] Klein and Criqui's projections lasted for weeks, as their Reclaiming the Monument project sought "to address the neglected historical and social narratives in our community . . . [by] utilizing light as a peaceful means of protest and resistance."[44] In historian Cox's assessment, the projections provided "the historical context that these Confederate icons long deserved."[45] Both commemorative and critical, generating ephemeral and enduring images, figurative highlighting illustrates how annotation as public protest interprets and also rewrites the memorial landscape.

CONTEXT AND ITS LIMITS

"Is the preservation of monuments," asks anthropologist Chelsey R. Carter, "more valuable than black people's lives?"[46] For defenders of the inherited memorial landscape dismissive of questions about symbols and social equity, one common rejoinder suggested by municipal commissions and local politicians is the creation of new interpretive resources. These signs and public markers—which we should view as notes added to texts of memory—attempt to (re)present a monument and its messages in light of disregarded truths and contemporary values. This type of annotation is called "contextualization." And, in my assessment, it is an ineffective compromise amid struggles to rewrite the nation's memorial landscape; or, as historian Thompson forewarns, "no amount of contextualizing signage will change most people's minds about statues."[47] Nonetheless, efforts to contextualize monuments are widespread and will continue, especially when a monument is relocated. Thus, it's useful that we review the limits of contextualized monuments and consider why these traces don't extend justice-directed re/marks.

We can appreciate, given aesthetics and authority, differences between Maya Little and her peers "adding historical context" to Silent Sam and, alternatively, annotators with political privilege contextualizing Confederate monuments to counterbalance racist messages. The former is figurative highlighting and resists white supremacy; the latter insufficiently redresses injustice etched into our memorial landscape. In *Monumental Harm*, constitutional law scholar Roger Hartley analyzes the contextualization of Confederate monuments, concluding "political and cultural realities in the contemporary South disqualify contextualization as a viable option."[48] Hartley evaluates context that augments standing monuments and identifies two reasons why it rarely is an "efficacious countermessage." First, words and images included on a new sign are often scrutinized, negotiated, and censored to appease white civic and business leaders, resulting in context that superficially addresses racial justice. And second, context is further restricted by a "dual heritage" ideology that posits Black and white Americans can each assert independent heritage claims deserving of equal respect. Consequently, Hartley notes that "whites end up largely controlling contextualization for they claim unilateral authority to determine when proposed content disparages Whites as a race."[49] In a complementary explanation about contextualization, Thompson describes "invisible force fields of legal protections" surrounding monuments that "repel attempts to add new signage that might point out the racist beliefs of the authorities who erected them."[50] Contextualization is annotation, yet annotators with ascribed cultural authority who mark Confederate monuments are not extending re/marks for their notes neither contest systemic racism nor advance more just social futures.

One oft-cited example of restricted contextualization is written on a sign beside the so-called Faithful Slave Memorial to Heyward Shepherd in West Virginia. Shepherd, a free Black man, was a railroad porter killed in 1859 during John Brown's raid at Harpers Ferry. In 1931, a large granite slab was dedicated in Shepherd's honor with text that reads, in part: "This boulder is erected by the Daughters of the Confederacy and the Sons of Confederate Veterans as a memorial to Heyward Shepherd, exemplifying the character and faithfulness of thousands of Negroes who, under many temptations throughout subsequent years of war, so conducted themselves that no stain was left upon a record which is the peculiar heritage of the American people, and an everlasting tribute to the best of both races." As a matter of fact, Shepherd was not enslaved and, moreover, the "Faithful Slave" narrative is a myth. Thus, in 1995, the National Parks Service added a sign that contextualizes the memorial, noting that "During the ceremony, voices raised to praise and denounce the monument." A section of the sign titled "Another Perspective" features W. E. B. Du Bois' 1932 commentary celebrating Brown who "aimed at human slavery a blow that woke a guilty nation." Nonetheless, local civil rights leaders remain upset because the sign does not debunk an injurious myth, whereas Confederate heritage groups decry the presence of any contextualization at all. As historian Caroline Janney details: "Today the Heyward Shepherd Memorial stands not as a representative of a community's collective remembrance, but rather as a testament to the struggle between Southern whites and African Americans to write their respective memories of the raid into the historical landscape."[51] Political barriers to contextualization also help us to understand why UNC students were ignored, in 2012, after demanding "the addition of a plaque" to Silent Sam,[52] and why Nashville park officials, after the 2019 "They Were Racists" highlighting, voted for a marker that never materialized.[53] Ultimately, contextualization is an impractical and inadequate response to Confederate monuments broadcasting white supremacy and racism.

Another useful object lesson in futile contextualization is offered by the Equestrian Statue of Theodore Roosevelt. The statue depicts Roosevelt, high on horseback, flanked by an African man on his left and a Native American man at right. It stood, for over eighty years, on public land in front of the American Museum of Natural History (AMNH) in New York City. During this time, public resistance to the statue included figurative highlighting with splattered red paint, first in 1971 and then again in 2017, as well as related Anti-Columbus Day Tours of the AMNH facilitated by Decolonize This Place from 2016 to 2019.[54] A 2018 report by the Mayoral Advisory Commission on City Art, Monuments, and Markers acknowledged the statue's "complex history" and reminded viewers that "height is power in public art, and Roosevelt's stature on his noble steed visibly expresses dominance and superiority over the Native American and African figures."[55]

The city's commission, however, did not recommend the statue's removal and only briefly noted contextualization as a possibility. One art critic, underwhelmed by the report's bureaucratic "half-measures," utilized the social vocabulary of annotation to state the obvious: "It doesn't require a sensitivity to subtexts to see that the composition, no matter how you gloss it, is quite literally an emblem of white-man-on-top."[56]

In 2019, following the city's report, the AMNH added three identical small plaques around the base of the equestrian statue. The plaques accompanied a short-term exhibit inside the museum, as well as additional online resources, because "we [AMNH] must recognize our country's enduring legacy of racial discrimination—as well as Roosevelt's troubling views on race. We must also acknowledge the Museum's own imperfect history."[57] The plaques beneath the statue stated: "This statue was unveiled to the public in 1940, as part of a larger New York State memorial to former N.Y. governor and U.S. President Theodore Roosevelt. Today, some see the statue as a heroic group; others, as a symbol of racial hierarchy. You can learn more about this statue inside the Museum and at [link]." A legal analysis of the monument's continued presence at the AMNH, published before its removal, described the contextualization as both "passive" and "the least impactful" method of addressing long-term controversy, noting: "The placards demonstrate the primary failing of passive contextualization, as they do not necessitate engagement. A passerby on the other side of the street could still see the *Equestrian Statue* without seeing these placards. Moreover, one cannot help but notice that these placards look temporary and out of place."[58] Indeed, this contextualization did not discourage yet another instance of figurative highlighting, in October of 2021, as red paint symbolically bloodied the plinth and the plaques.[59] The resulting palimpsest, to my eye, encapsulates the hybridity of contrasting public re/marks and the critical rejection of colonialist ideology.

Despite contextualization, the Equestrian Statue of Theodore Roosevelt was removed from the AMNH in early 2022, and the plinth a few months later. Today, two plaques mark the ground where it stood. One honors Roosevelt, the other mentions revised public memory: "The Equestrian Statue of Theodore Roosevelt erected on this site by New York State following Roosevelt's death was removed in 2022 by agreement among the Museum, the Roosevelt family, and the City of New York because its composition suggested a racial hierarchy." The verb "suggested" further conveys the

4.6 A plaque added by the American Museum of Natural History to the Equestrian Statue of Theodore Roosevelt splattered with red paint, 2021. Courtesy of Hakim Bishara/ *Hyperallergic.*

limits of contextualization and appeasement to those in power, for this plaque neither concedes prior offense nor signals toward social justice. In 2026, the equestrian statue is to be displayed at the Theodore Roosevelt Presidential Library, in the small town of Medora, North Dakota.[60] The library's board accepts that the statue "is problematic in its composition;" accordingly, it will establish an Advisory Council "composed of representatives of the Indigenous Tribal and Black communities, historians, scholars, and artists to guide the recontextualization of the statue."[61] Passive contextualization failed in New York City. We shall see how this statue—with another iteration of context—rewrites rural North Dakota's memorial landscape. Whatever happens, this marked monument illustrates the difficulty of adding notes to an inherently problematic text in the hopes of reinterpreting artistic and historical complexity.

Should you read an explanatory sign, added to a controversial monument by annotators with cultural and political authority, it's unlikely to change your comprehension of the memorial landscape. We should not expect contextual notes to meaningfully alter problematic messages communicated by offensive monuments. Unlike figurative highlighting, I maintain that adding contextualization to a monument is not a viable means of advancing more just social change.

"SHOW US WHAT YOUR MONUMENT WOULD LOOK LIKE"

Author Clint Smith opens *How the Word Is Passed* in his hometown of New Orleans, along the marge of the Mississippi River, reading a marker about the transatlantic slave trade: "In recent years, markers like this began to go up throughout the city, each documenting a specific area's relationship to enslavement—part of a broader reckoning."[62] The particular marker was erected in early 2018 amid a broader reckoning that rewrote the city's memorial landscape. Months before the marker appeared, local third-graders went about the city reading statues, noticing signs, and discussing Confederate monuments. Then they wrote a book with their re/marks.

In the spring of 2017, over a period of twenty-six days, four monuments valorizing the Confederacy and its Lost Cause myth were removed from public settings in New Orleans.[63] The Battle of Liberty Place Monument was the first to go; it commemorated an 1874 insurrection by white supremacists. The next was a statue of Jefferson Davis, president of the Confederacy, followed by a monument honoring General P. G. T. Beauregard. And on May 19, the towering bronze figure of Robert E. Lee, standing atop a sixty-foot marble column, was removed by workers wearing bullet-proof vests and clothing that disguised their identity. That spring, one third-grade class from Homer A. Plessy Community School in the French Quarter visited these monuments and other markers across the city. They also studied the Civil War, as educator Amy Dickerson told me, to learn "who these people [were] that we see in the statues across the city [and] what were they fighting for."[64] And the students considered "who or what people, places, things, ideas, or events would be appropriate for commemorating in a public space."[65] After their classroom and community-based inquiry, and with support from the nonprofit literacy organization 826 New Orleans, Dickerson's students published *Courageous, Eccentric, Diverse: New Monuments for New Orleans* in the fall of 2017, just six months after the four monuments were carted away. *Courageous, Eccentric, Diverse* is an insightful response to a changed community. It is also a template for how young annotators can mark monuments with traces we will understand as critical, creative, and civic re/marks.

"They learned how to read art and interpret art," Dickerson reminisced about her former students. "Not just paintings, but statues, sculptures, anything that was in front of them. We always started everything we did with, 'What do you notice? What do you wonder?'" Listening to Dickerson, I heard the unmistakable echo of civil rights activist and art historian Freeman H. M. Murray, author of the influential book *Emancipation and the Freed in American Sculpture*. Published a century before Dickerson's students reimagined their city's statues, Murray's book encouraged readers to interpret works of art "from our own peculiar viewpoint" by asking: "What does it mean? What does it suggest? What impression is it likely to make on those who view it? What will be the effect on present-day problems, of its obvious and also of its insidious teachings?"[66] Murray's questions are as pertinent today as they were in 1916, and they can help us read the twenty-one "persuasive proposals for new monuments" featured in *Courageous, Eccentric, Diverse*. In one respect, the students' book affirms more recent educational research suggesting that children who study their city's monuments can develop critical literacies and design multimodal "monuments

4.7 Monument for Mahalia Jackson by student Taliyah Byers in *Courageous, Eccentric, Diverse*. Courtesy of 826 New Orleans.

Mules

TERRELL HILL

Mules deserve monuments because they are beautiful animals. I love mules. They do their jobs. They don't just sit around in the wild, they take people on tours in the French Quarter. They pull heavy, heavy carriages. Mules are hybrids. A hybrid is a horse and a donkey combined. They don't use horses for carriages because they have thick fur and they don't do well because they get really hot and sweaty. Mules do better because they are a hybrid of horses and donkeys. They don't have that much fur. They stick their tongues out a lot. In New Orleans they feed them and give them water, not like in New York. My favorite mule is Snoball because she has a pretty white fur coat that is really soft. Mules deserve a monument because they like hot weather. Mules are almost a heavy horse. They are great and stinky. Go see them in person at Jackson Square in New Orleans.

4.8 Monument for Mules by student Terrell Hill in *Courageous, Eccentric, Diverse*. Courtesy of 826 New Orleans.

to honor collective action for humanity."[67] What you will also notice is that *Courageous, Eccentric, Diverse* celebrates children's monumental creativity as a testament to how they can broadcast annotated visions of a more just memorial landscape.

Students proposed monuments for notable New Orleanians like Mahalia Jackson and Trombone Shorty, animals including mules and crawfish, as well as beignets and magnolias, and The Houma Nation who, as one student wrote: "deserve a monument because they are fighting against global warming and coastal erosion."[68] Every entry in *Courageous, Eccentric, Diverse* features two components created by each student: persuasive writing about the new monument; and artwork displaying it in the memorial landscape. And students' monumental art is the result of annotation, for their proposals are placed atop pedestals abandoned at Liberty Place, as well as by Jefferson, Beauregard, and Lee. Dickerson's students visited the controversial monuments while they stood. Once removed, collaborators with 826 New Orleans photographed the empty pedestals. After writing their proposals, students selected one of the four pictures as a canvas upon which they drew images, collaged figures of people and animals, wrote words and phrases, and marked up well-known settings with original visions. When the project began, Dickerson hadn't planned for students to publish a book about the city's monuments, nor was she teaching creative annotation strategies. Yet what we see in *Courageous, Eccentric, Diverse* is the result of student annotators "drawing pictures of their proposed monuments, and mounting them on photographs of the empty spaces where the Confederate monuments once stood."[69] The synthesis of hand-drawn art atop a photographed scene produces re/marks about the familiar as speculative. Collectively, students' new images present a civic composition whereby everyday spaces are more inviting, humorous, and dignified. When I asked Dickerson how she guided students to create their annotated images, she replied simply: "We just let them have creative freedom. The only thing we said was, 'Show us what your monument would look like.'"

Just as author Smith read a marker to help write about slavery and public memory, so, too, did nine-year-old student Abigail Matthews. A self-described "cool, smart, and funny" kid, Matthews astutely read a local marker during one class field trip; and her comprehension of memorialization, controversy, and justice subsequently informed her proposed monument. "We went on a walking field trip in the French Quarter one day," Dickerson told me, "and there is a tiny little marker at the end of Esplanade Avenue. That is the only historical marker to say, 'This is where Solomon Northup was sold and bought.'" According to the inscription, it marks "the former site of Theophilus Freeman's notorious slave pen (demolished after the Civil War) where Solomon Northup, a free man of color from New York, was sold into slavery in 1841. Northup's story is chronicled in his 1853 memoir *12 Years a Slave* and in the award winning movie by the same name." In early 2017, when Matthews and her peers read that marker, it was the only one along Esplanade Avenue (in 2018, a marker about the city's role in the domestic slave trade was added across the street and complements the transatlantic slave trade marker noted by Smith). Here is how Dickerson remembers Matthews reading and then beginning to understand the difference between history and memory:

We stood at that marker. And she asked question after question after question. And connected it to, 'This is the only thing here. It's just this little plaque that you can read talking about what happened here and this amazing person who just got a movie made about his incredible life and experience.' I remember her saying, 'People are mad that Confederate heroes are being removed. Why? This doesn't make any sense. Those people [Confederates] were hurting people like him [Northup]. And we're celebrating those people. They have statues. Not just

4.9 Solomon Northup "12 Years a Slave" place marker in New Orleans with "Black Man" graffiti. Courtesy of Infrogmation of New Orleans.

statues. Humongous statues! But this guy just gets a little plaque like that.' She really connected all that. It really made her think.

Matthews' contribution to *Courageous, Eccentric, Diverse* is a proposed monument for Solomon Northup. Her essay summarizes information she read on the Esplanade Avenue marker, including—in her words—that Northup "wrote a book about his life" and that this "book became into a movie that was filmed in New Orleans." Matthews appears to have also conducted research about Northup, for her entry mentions: "When he was a slave, he helped other slaves. He also helped slaves to read and write. He helped other slaves even though it was against the law." And there is yet another notable feature of her essay, for Matthews wrote about the value of visiting and reading the memorial landscape: "If his monument is ever built, then you should also go see his statue. If there is a caption on the bottom then you can also see all the great things Solomon Northup has done." As you look at Matthews' artwork, notice the three re/marks written directly onto the photograph of the traffic circle once occupied by Beauregard.

4.10 Monument for Solomon Northup by student Abigail Matthews in *Courageous, Eccentric, Diverse*. Courtesy of 826 New Orleans.

Two notes address the public memory of Northup: "A true HERO!" and "Solomon Northup rest in peace!" Distinctively, Matthews wrote the third annotation as if it were spoken by Northup regarding his legacy: "Fighting against slavery is my only job!" Dickerson also shared with me why Matthews, as an annotator, selected this particular monument: "She put hers on Beauregard. She said it was because he was a general. So he was fighting to keep slavery. And so that's why she put Solomon Northup, her memorial, on General Beauregard." Matthews marked a Confederate monument and, by commemorating Northup, made visible a more just counternarrative.

Monuments are texts of memory that mark land and legacy. The US memorial landscape is neither a given nor necessarily a public good—and whether this part of our built environment is revered or reviled or reimagined, it will be marked. You may balk at figurative highlighting as transgressive, or celebrate these re/marks of ideological resistance. And you may be dispirited by the bureaucratic limits of contextualization, or see interpretive signs as a pragmatic compromise to preserve art as educational artifacts. We can, however, agree that both types of notes will continue augmenting public monuments as annotators comment on how the inherited past is broadcast into the future. And we should also commend the twenty-one authors of *Courageous, Eccentric, Diverse*, like Abigail Matthews, as well as educator Amy Dickerson and her 826 New Orleans colleagues, for showing us how children can reconfigure commemoration. The book exemplifies a critical stance toward literacy given how students read their city's history, identified what Freeman Murray called the "insidious teachings" of statues, and then (re)presented new alternatives. *Courageous, Eccentric, Diverse* is also an expression that creatively blends together words, images, and annotation to communicate more inclusive figures and futures. The *National Monument Audit* concludes with a call to "envision a landscape that reflects a plurality of stories and histories, where monuments serve as waystations along a bending arc of justice."[70] In New Orleans, we know what those justice-directed waystations may look like thanks to third-graders who reclaimed abandoned pedestals with monumental re/marks of compassion and creativity.

5

BOOK MARKS

We are annotators who can circulate activism and affirmation.

"One of the most active things you can do to a book," author Alex Gino told me, "is to literally change the book for the next person who reads it. To engage with it. To leave your mark on it. With a marker."[1] Gino writes queer and progressive middle grade novels. They are also an annotator. On July 1, 2021, Gino posted a "reminder" on Twitter, stating: "You officially have my permission to correct your copy of Melissa's Story. Yes, the cover is beautiful. Part of trans justice is to accept that your sense of 'beauty' doesn't matter if someone need to change their appearance to be themself. #SharpieActivism."[2] The tweet's picture shows Gino, black Sharpie in hand, crossing through the title of their book and writing, atop the cover, "Melissa's Story." The re/marks of #SharpieActivism quickly appeared across social media, at libraries, and in schools. Annotators embraced Gino's request for handwritten book-marking by emending the title, adding colorful lettering and drawings across the cover, and amplifying #SharpieActivism.

Gino's lauded debut novel was initially published as *George* in 2015. About a week after their 2021 #SharpieActivism tweet, Gino shared a blog post in which they acknowledged "a big mistake" and apologized to their character Melissa, "the larger trans community," and readers.[3] "I think the disconnect between the name George and the pronoun she is a valuable literary technique and reflects the tension many trans people feel, especially before coming out to others," Gino wrote. "But on the cover? It is an unequivocal error. Using a person's name is a basic form of respect, and I failed my main character." Protagonist Melissa is a fourth-grader whose family, friends, classmates, and teachers all perceive—and also all refer to her—as a boy named George. In this coming-of-age story, we follow Melissa encountering challenges and finding recognition for who she is as a transgender girl. In addition to the book's many distinctions—it won the esteemed Stonewall Award from the American Library Association (ALA) and has been translated into over a dozen languages—the ALA's Office for Intellectual Freedom first included Gino's novel on its "Top 10 Most Challenged Books Lists" in 2016. In 2019, for instance, the book topped that list as it was "challenged, banned, restricted, and hidden to avoid controversy; for LGBTQIA+ content and a transgender character; because schools and libraries should not 'put books in a child's hand that require discussion'; for sexual references; and for conflicting with a religious viewpoint and 'traditional family structure.'"[4] From 2018 to 2020, it was the most censored book in America.

During the summer of 2021 and well into the new academic year, annotators joined #SharpieActivism en masse. Educators, librarians, parents, and young readers imaginatively marked Gino's book as "Melissa's Story," and then shared pictures and videos of their corrected copies across Twitter, TikTok, and Instagram.[5] "I was finally able to do this on my first day back in the classroom," tweeted Joy Kirr, a middle grade literacy educator in Illinois.[6] School librarian Jane Hill posted an image with over two dozen marked books, writing, "I tried to use my best handwriting for our class set."[7] When Gino spoke with me about #SharpieActivism, they emphasized that "the purpose of activism is to invoke change" and concluded, "It's a successful campaign. In the purest sense of trying to create a change." Gino's publisher supported that change, too. Scholastic announced the book would be retitled *Melissa* and reprinted with a new cover in the spring of 2022.[8] Gino publicized the change, noting: "What we call people matters and we all deserve to be referred to in ways that feel good to us. Calling the book *Melissa* is a way to respect her, as well as all transgender people. The text inside won't change, so the name George will still appear to reflect the character's growth within the novel, but Melissa will be the first name readers will know her by. I hope you'll make the change with us."[9]

Melissa appeared on bookshelves in April of 2022, just as PEN America released *Banned in the USA*, a report about censorship in American public schools. The report examined book banning over the prior nine months, a period of time that coincided with #SharpieActivism and the printing of *Melissa*. PEN America documented "a profound increase in both the number of books banned and the intense focus on books that relate to communities of color and LGBTQ+ subjects," as evidenced by over one thousand unique book titles banned, removed from school libraries, prohibited in classrooms, or pulled from circulation during investigations.[10] Among those books, common themes reflected debates about the teaching of race and racism, LGBTQIA+ identities, and sexual education. Unsurprisingly, *Melissa* is featured in the report, illustrative of a trend: "Titles that deal explicitly with LGBTQ+ topics, or have LGBTQ+ protagonists or prominent secondary characters have been a major target in the current wave of book bans." While—as we will read—some school librarians wrote "Melissa's Story" across book covers and participated in #SharpieActivism throughout the 2021–22 school year, *Melissa* was also marked by censorship when banned by six school districts in Florida and three in Texas, as well as by districts in Oklahoma and Pennsylvania. During the 2022–23 academic year, *Melissa* was also banned by districts in Nebraska, North Carolina, and South Carolina.[11]

Gino is quoted in *Banned in the USA* addressing a central fallacy of book censorship: "Hiding the beautiful range of humanity from young people does not keep young people from being themselves." Ultimately, they assert, "positive representation saves lives." PEN America recently reported data covering both the 2021–22 and 2022–23 school years, identifying 5,894 titles banned in thirty-three states.[12] This growing censorship movement is augmented by educational gag orders, such as Florida's so-called "Don't Say Gay" law, which restrict what can be discussed in schools. The result, according to PEN America, is disconcerting: "Students have First Amendment rights to access information and ideas in schools, and these bans and legislative shifts pose clear threats to those rights."[13] As I write, *Melissa* remains among the twenty most banned books in American schools.

5.1 Alex Gino's signature—a book mark—added to my first edition copy of *Melissa*, originally published as *George* in 2015. Photograph by author (2023).

#SHARPIEACTIVISM AS A QUEER INTERVENTION

Our careful reading of #SharpieActivism is timely in light of two troubling realities: Books with LGBTQIA+ topics and characters are being banned in public schools; and, outside of school, discriminatory anti-trans legislation has banned or is threatening gender affirming care, drag performances, youth participation in sports, and people's legal recognition.[14] Granted, it is notable that many individuals honored Gino's call for correction—readers annotated book covers, shared justice-aligned posts on social media, and advocated for affirming youth literature. It's also encouraging that one of the world's largest publishers of children's books responded receptively to grassroots activism and printed *Melissa* because readers publicly marked books with re/marks about trans justice. Nonetheless, you might be inclined to minimize this instance of annotation-powered activism on account of persistent anti-LGTBQIA+ rhetoric and legislation. Moreover, it may not be immediately evident how #SharpieActivism galvanized a collective effort to mark books with notes as a means of addressing broader gender justice concerns. In other words, how did #SharpieActivism extend annotator re/marks?

I respond to this question by uplifting public and school librarians who, as annotators, creatively shaped #SharpieActivism within the familiar literacy setting of the library. Libraries, according to librarian—and recent ALA president—Emily Drabinski, are "sites constructed by the disciplinary power of language."[15] Given our interest in the literacies of annotation, we should consider how librarians in a setting constructed by the power of language marked a book about the contingency of names and identities, joined efforts to revise that book's title, and boosted an online campaign organized around a hashtag denoting material and social change. To do so, I center Drabinski's advocacy for "a queer library politics" as one pragmatic response to how libraries organize and share knowledge. In her article "Queering the Catalog," Drabinski reviews library cataloging practices as historically and structurally biased, yet she argues that corrective efforts are often functional but not transformative. Alternatively, she suggests that queer perspectives can invite both librarians and patrons into a "project of dialogic pedagogical interventions" whereby library practices, like classification, become sites of struggle and resistance. Because of librarians, I contend it is appropriate to discuss #SharpieActivism as a *queer intervention*, or what Drabinski defines as a form of engagement that aims to "highlight and make visible the contingency of cataloging decisions."[16] It's instructive to quote Drabinski at length regarding this form of public pedagogy for we can appreciate how it relates to re/marks. Specifically, queer interventions:

leave intact the traces of historicity and ideology that mar the classification and cataloging project. Such traces can reveal the limit of the universal knowledge organization project, inviting technical interventions that highlight the constructed nature of classification structures and controlled vocabularies. These traces also represent moments when the burden of undoing the hegemony of library classification and cataloging shifts from the back office to the reference desk and classroom, where public service librarians can intervene and emphasize the discursivity of classification and cataloging by engaging in critical reflection with users about what they do and do not see in the library catalog.[17]

We will study social media posts by public and school librarians to perceive #SharpieActivism as a queer and pedagogical intervention. Librarians are annotators who routinely mark books. #SharpieActivism displayed librarians' enduring re/marks of resistance, or what Drabinski refers to as "remnants." As you read, notice how remnants written across book covers and social media made ideology visible and helped readers, whether in the library or online, "consider how the organization of, and access to, knowledge is politically and socially produced."[18]

In the next section, I begin our discussion by drawing from the library and information science (LIS) literature to review how libraries have classified and physically marked books. I suggest that we read #SharpieActivism—as a queer intervention—within a broader historical context of dominant cataloging decisions for, per Drabinski, such practices often "fail to accurately and respectfully organize library materials about social groups and identities that lack social and political power."[19] I will then show how #SharpieActivism extended collective participation in critical librarianship practices as public libraries circulated, among local communities and online networks, annotated copies of *Melissa* and assertive counternarratives about LGBTQIA+ justice. And, finally, we'll meet three school librarians who shared #SharpieActivism re/marks with their students. The varied approaches and experiences of these librarians demonstrate how justice-directed librarianship practices were augmented by critical and creative annotation.

PZ7.1.G576 GEO 2015

How is *Melissa* marked at your local library? And what marks accompany other books about trans individuals and topics?

I wrote most of this book around the corner from the central hub of the Cambridge Public Library (CPL) in Massachusetts. Known locally as the Main Library, I regularly visited the third floor Children's Room with my toddler; and, one spring afternoon, I wandered from the picture books over to "Fiction, Alphabetical by Author." Every copy of *Melissa* was marked by CPL librarians with three annotations on the cover, two on the book's spine, and one inside. Here's what I noticed. A barcode was stuck atop the cover's upper left corner to assist with circulation as patrons borrowed and returned the book; a librarian informed me that the initial "3" indicated an item and the next "1189" associated the item with the CPL system. "George" was struck-through with a large black "X" across all the covers.

5.2 Annotated copies of *Melissa* by Alex Gino on the shelf at the Cambridge Public Library in Cambridge, Massachusetts. Photograph by author (2023).

The handwritten addition of "Melissa's Story" appeared on every copy in block letters matching the same colors of the original design—red, orange, yellow, green, blue, and violet, the six colors of the pride flag. The spine of each book displayed a custom printed "Melissa's Story" label with similar colors. And, at the bottom of the spine, each book was marked "J FIC GIN" to classify the book as juvenile fiction and order the book on the shelf alphabetically by "Gino." Another CPL mark was inside the front cover—a circular stamp labeled "Cambridge Public Library" and also "Juvenile Dept.," with "4/16" written inside the circle, noting that CPL acquired this copy in April of 2016. While some of these annotations are unique to *Melissa*, it's unremarkable to observe that libraries mark books.

You can easily locate books on the shelves of libraries because of *classification*. And, crucially, the literacy practice of annotation complements the library practice of classification.[20] Classification, in broad terms, is the practice of organizing items, like books, into classes based upon shared characteristics and then ordering classes into a logical, and often hierarchical, structure that is comprehensive and contemporary. In *Sorting Things Out*, scholars Geoffrey Bowker and Susan Star describe classifications as "powerful technologies" of our built information environments, like libraries. However, these typical and often invisible technologies are not neutral, for "each standard and each category valorizes some point of view and silences another. This is not inherently a bad thing—indeed it is inescapable. But it *is* an ethical choice, and as such it is dangerous."[21] Library scholar Hope Olson offers a similar observation in *The Power to Name* regarding knowledge organization: "The classifications that we use in libraries are intended to be universal, but are actually culturally specific;" furthermore, Olson mentions that "classifications reflect the mainstream society in which they are created with all of its ideologies and biases."[22] Ideological and biased, yes, though classifying books is necessary and purposeful, according to classification scholar Melissa Adler, who offers an accessible summary:

Bibliographic classification in libraries has a distinct meaning and purpose, which concerns the physical location of library materials, that is, the placement of items on library shelves. Think of it as a geographical code. A class determines the call number—the notation stamped on the spine of the volume and in the corresponding catalog record, directing patrons to the book. A class also brings topically related materials together—a process called collocation—ideally placing similar books in the same section, according to where they fit within a given discipline. Bibliographic classification can be conceived of as a sorting mechanism—a way of drawing associations and relationships across methodologically or substantively similar things.[23]

Globally, the most prevalent "sorting mechanism" is the Dewey Decimal Classification (DDC) system, first published in 1876. In the US, the Library of Congress Classification (LCC) system, developed between 1899 and 1903, is now primarily used by research and academic libraries.[24] Both schemes assign books to classes based on subject or discipline and then further group books by specific topics. Once a book is classified, it's assigned *notation*—or a call number—an alphanumeric representation of the class plus information about the author and publication year.[25] And, as Alder writes, that call number is "stamped on the spine of the volume." You have read book call numbers as a library patron. And we will recognize bibliographic notation as a form of annotation because call numbers literally mark books.

Our attention to how libraries classify LGBTQIA+ books is usefully directed by Drabinski's review of these practices from a queer perspective. She concludes: "Dominant classification structures represent materials about gender and sexuality in ways that are inaccurate at best and discriminatory at worst."[26] The development of DDC is illustrative. The thirteenth edition of DDC, from 1932, was the first to mention "Homosexuality" with notation 132.7546, classified among "Sexual perversions" including bestiality and incest, and organized within "Sexual manias and aberrations" as a subclass of "Derangements leading to vice." *DDC 13* also classified "Homosexuality" at 159.9734846 within an "Alternativ" [sic] psychology scheme "based on current lines of thought."[27] DDC's use of "perversions" persisted for decades; in 1965, for instance, *DDC 17* listed call number 301.415 "Sex life outside marriage" for books about "Concubinage, premarital relations, adultery, prostitution, homosexuality and other perversions."[28] In 1980, librarian Sanford Berman—the prominent activist and author credited with transforming cataloging practice—published an "indictment" of *DDC 19*. Berman criticized notation 306.7 "Institutions pertaining to relations of the sexes," and wrote: "It continues the unpardonable neglect of Gays by again assigning only *one* five-digit spot to 'Homosexuality,' making no provision for the independent collocation of materials dealing uniquely with Gay men, Lesbians, and the Gay Liberation Movement. Moreover, 'Bisexuality' has been ineptly subsumed under 'Homosexuality,' while 'Transvestism,' 'Transsexuality,' and 'Heterosexuality,' all ignored in Edition 18, similarly appear nowhere in *DDC 19*."[29] The twenty-third, and current, edition of DDC was published in 2011. In 2018, librarian Violet Fox (a DDC editor at the time) helped establish 306.76 "Sexual orientation, transgender identity, intersexuality" as a "clear place for interdisciplinary resources about the LGBT community as a whole."[30] This effort included an explicit provision to class "works about Gender nonconformity and Gender nonconforming people at 306.768 Transgender identity and intersexuality." This update also revised the scheme's inherited and derogatory terminology: "Transgender identity" replaced "Transgenderism;" "Transgender people" replaced "Transgenderists;" and "Transgendered people" was removed. While necessary decisions, Drabinski reminds us such cataloging corrections are imperfect given the contingency of identity, for it is "in the text of the classification itself where we can see heteronormativity written into the order of things."[31]

Beyond DDC, the problematic ideologies of bibliographic classification are thoroughly documented by librarians and LIS scholars. For example, LCC classifies books about "The Family. Marriage. Women" using the

DECIMAL CLASIFICATION

132.6 Derangements leading to crime   Criminal manias
See also 132.223 Moral imbecility. For legal responsibility see 340.6 Medical jurisprudence, 347.1 Legal capacity

.62   Kleptomania

.63   Pathologic swindlers

.64   Destructiv manias: pyromania

.65   Homicidal and suicidal manias

.7   Derangements leading to vice   Vicious manias
See also 132.223 Moral imbecility

.72   Dipsomania
See also 132.161 Alcoholism, 178 Temperance, 616.861 Alcoholism from medical viewpoint

.73   Drug addiction
Morphinomania or morphinism, cocainomania, etheromania etc

.74   Pathologic lying

.75   Sexual manias and aberraticns
Including those leading to crime. Sexual anomalies, sexual psychopaths. See also 176 Sexual ethics

.752   Eroticism   Erotic delusions

.753   Nymphomania

.754   Sexual perversions

I	General questions	6	Sexual inversion Homo-
2	Exhibitionism		sexuality
3	Fetishism	7	Incest
4	Masochism Sadism	8	Masturbation
5	Bestiality	9	Other

.755   Moral impotence   Frigidity

.8   Mnemonic derangements   Memory defects
Not knowing in one state what past in another. See also 154 Memory

.82   Hypermnesia

5.3 Classification 132.7546, including "Homosexuality" in section for "Sexual perversions." *Decimal Classification and Relativ Index* by Melvil Dewey, Edition 13, 1932.

subclass HQ, as H refers to the broader class of Social Sciences. According to Adler, we should read HQ as a "a highly contested space," for "the first edition of the *Library of Congress Classification*, printed in 1910, placed homosexuality within 'Abnormal sex relations.'"[32] The mark of this classification, on shelves and as stigma, persisted well after LCC policy changed in 1972: "Erasing the hierarchical relationship from the classification system did not, however, alter the arrangement of books on the shelves," Adler details, "and changing indentation in the printed classification did not wipe away the legacy of the previous structure."[33] Today, another problematic detail of HQ is the range HQ77.7—HQ77.9, revised in 2016, which

5.4 Books, annotated with call numbers and other labels, assigned DDC 306.768 "Transgender identity and intersexuality." Photograph by author (2023).

classifies books about "Transsexualism. Transgenderism." The term "transsexualism," notes scholar Claire McDonald Indermaur, "is considered to be an outdated—and often offensive—term by many transgender individuals."[34] The continued use of this term is among the criticisms advanced by cataloger librarian K. R. Roberto whose research shows how classification establishes "normative boundaries for queer sexualities and gender" and "library environments that are passively hostile to transgender users."[35] Classification—the traces of which you read as annotated call numbers—structures our physical spaces and social discourses, resulting in marked books and regulated identities. And libraries must classify books, of course, for the alternative is a large pile of disorganized paper, yet doing so produces marks both helpful and harmful. This bibliographic practice will endure, just as ongoing revision to DDC and LCC will be a needed yet insufficient fix; as Adler concedes: "Simply changing the classifications fails to address the larger challenges that both librarians and queer activists face as they negotiate the dilemmas of classification for access."[36]

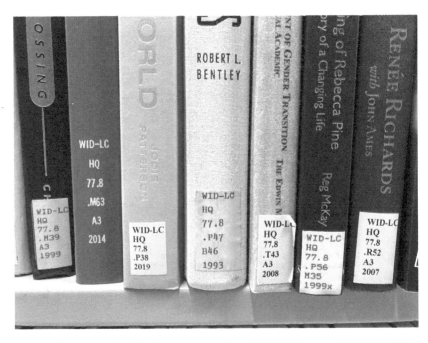

5.5 Books, annotated with call numbers, assigned within LCC range HQ77.7—HQ77.9 "Transsexualism. Transgenderism." Photograph by author (2023).

The copies of *Melissa* that I located at CPL were labeled "J FIC GIN" for the library uses DDC to classify juvenile fiction and arrange books alphabetically on the shelf. When it was first published, the Library of Congress also classified Gino's book as "PZ7.1.G576 Geo 2015." We would, for example, find copies of the book assigned this call number at a university library used by future teachers and librarians. Let's read the LCC call number together. Subclass PZ7 refers to "Juvenile belles lettres" (within class P for Language and Literature), the ".1" indicates the book was published in or after 2015, ".G576" identifies Gino as the author (using what's known as a Cutter Number, for all of their books are labeled with ".G576"), "Geo" references the title *George* and "2015" is the publication year. To its credit, the Library of Congress provides an authority file for *Melissa* that lists, as variants, both *George* and "Melissa's story."[37] And "PZ7.1.G576 Mel 2022" is associated with the 2022 printing of *Melissa* as a new edition. Yet the trace "Geo" remains written as an enduring mark of the book's first classification. This codifies a fixed call number—despite Gino's insistence that "calling the book *Melissa* is a way to respect her, as well as all transgender people"—and further illustrates Drabinski's point: "Our catalogs and classification structures are themselves technologies of power, facilitating some ways of knowing and not others, representing certain ideological ways of seeing the world, and, crucially, not others."[38] Because we find "Geo" in a call number marked by heteronormative ideology, it's vital to also read the book's annotated cover as a re/mark of resistance, as the remnant of a queer intervention, that expands people's engagement with library catalogs and liberatory possibilities.

"JUST LIKE THAT!"

"It's very true to the trans experience," Gino mentioned to me, commenting on readers changing the name of their book, "to have been known as one thing, and to have to ask people to change it. To ask people to do something they don't usually do. And do something that maybe even feels against the rules." Gino's insistence that people "do something they don't usually do" echoes advocacy by Drabinski for *critical librarianship*, which acknowledges that "things could be different from the way they are now."[39] There are many interpretations of critical librarianship and related efforts cannot be reduced to a single concept or technique; as librarian David Ketchum recently wrote: "Librarians have most certainly been practicing critical librarianship without a label or definition for a very long time."[40] For Drabinski, however, a critical approach means librarians "can respond nimbly" to societal problems visibly reflected on library shelves. Such a stance is pertinent to our understanding of how public libraries annotated *Melissa* and circulated justice-oriented re/marks as a queer intervention: "Critical librarians acknowledge the contingency and constructedness of the world we find ourselves living and working in. Simply because things have 'always been this way' does not mean they are meant to be or that they will be forever. For the critical librarian, nothing about the ways things are is a given, and all is subject to change."[41] And we can readily recognize traces of that change in #SharpieActivism.

Critical librarianship practices are evident in social media tagged with #SharpieActivism. Public libraries amplified the social relevance of annotation, and the social necessity of activism, by posting creative covers, supportive messages, and affirming hashtags. Less than a week after Gino's July 2021 post about "Melissa's Story," the Garden Home Community Library in Oregon tweeted: "You might notice that we've 'defaced' a book in our collection. For the backstory, read author Alex Gino's blog post encouraging people to alter their copies with a little #sharpieactivism."[42] Two days later, the North Canton Public Library, just outside Akron, Ohio, shared a similar tweet: "Did we really just write on a library book? Yup. Why? The author asked us to!"[43] On Instagram, the Bloomfield Public Library, located near Hartford, Connecticut, shared selections from Gino's blog post alongside video of a librarian marking two copies of the book while standing at a circulation desk. The library's post featured multiple tags, including #weserveall, #transpride, and the locally relevant #comebloomwithus.[44] And during Banned Books Week that fall—the annual event celebrating the freedom to read and open access to information—Buncombe County Public Libraries in North Carolina took to Instagram and shared a colorful collage of marked books from six different youth librarians, commenting: "Check out Mx. Gino's post on #sharpieactivism and share your own corrected cover!"[45] That post used hashtags advocating for both trans youth (#transpride, #bewhoyouare) and their literacies (#teenlibrary, #readmore). Though most of these posts didn't go viral, one exception was a TikTok video shared by Lyons Falls Library, in rural upstate New York, that garnered over 339,000 views. The ten-second video shows before-and-after pictures of a Sharpied book, overlaid with text that reads: "When an author realizes their mistake and tells people to change the cover and you're an inclusive library." We should commend public libraries that not only marked *Melissa* but then chose to broadcast re/marks about who is welcome in the library and whose stories should be celebrated. These posts are accessible remnants indicating how libraries collectively contributed to a queer intervention.

Participation in #SharpieActivism also showed how feasible it was for librarians to "respond nimbly" with simple tools and caring gestures as a part of their daily practice. One TikTok video, posted two weeks after Gino tweeted their "reminder" to correct the book, encapsulates what Drabinski refers to as the importance of librarians facilitating "a liberatory practice in all the quotidian aspects of our work, which, if we are honest, is most of

BOOK MARKS   109

5.6 Screenshot of a #SharpieActivism TikTok video with *Melissa* displayed at a library. Courtesy of Lyons Falls Library.

library work."⁴⁶ The video was shared by Stoughton Public Library, located near Madison, Wisconsin, and shows a librarian changing the cover of the book's digital audiobook version. Only seventeen-seconds long, we see the librarian using scissors to cut out a "Melissa's Story" cover, which is then taped as a label onto the audiobook's case.⁴⁷ Throughout the video, we hear Lizzo's song "Like a Girl." Stoughton Public Library's video also incorporates the common TikTok element of overlaid text, yet another form of annotation, including a concise description of the librarian's actions,

5.7 Screenshot of a #SharpieActivism TikTok video with a librarian changing the cover of the digital audiobook version of *Melissa*. Courtesy of Stoughton Public Library.

the introductory note "Fixing a mistake.," and finally an emphatic "Just Like That!" When posted, the video was augmented with ten hashtags, four of which referenced gender justice: #weseeyou, #goodbyedeadname, #bewhoyouare, and #transgirlsaregirls.[48] The library's TikTok account has posted over 120 videos since 2021, most of which are short and humorous day-at-the-library sketches, with a handful that capture the quotidian aspects of librarianship: unboxing books, putting a protective cover on a new book, and affixing tape to the spines of books. With both creativity and compassion, Stoughton Public Library's #SharpieActivism video demonstrates how—"Just Like That!"—the unremarkable tasks of librarianship can become liberatory moments that extend the social life of a book and signal a more just social future.

Earlier, I questioned how we should read #SharpieActivism as a movement that extended re/marks. Prior to the enthusiastic marking of *Melissa*, critical approaches to librarianship had made progress creating more gender-inclusive library policies, advancing LGBTQIA+ cataloging and collection development initiatives, and establishing programming to affirm rainbow families.[49] Our brief survey of social media posts shows how, over the course of a few months in the summer and fall of 2021, an emergent collective of public libraries refashioned one routine aspect of librarianship—the marking of books—into critical and justice-directed activism. This corpus of annotation represents a noteworthy departure from libraries' typical social media content, like event announcements, as evidenced by creatively handwritten covers paired with carefully selected hashtags (i.e. #transpride, #bewhoyouare, #transgirlsaregirls). Moreover, the apparent simplicity of #SharpieActivism should not obscure the more nuanced hybridity of this queer intervention. We see three important visual elements on annotated book covers: first, the referent "George," which often remains partly visible; second, a large "X," strike-through, series of lines, or scribbles atop the prior title, often with a black marker, as bold re/marks of resistance; and third, the addition of "Melissa's Story," as well as other words and images (like the trans pride flag), to further comment on needed narratives of trans belonging and justice. It's important that these varied annotations all appear together, creating a layered composition, for queer interventions do not entirely erase the evidence of dominant ideology but, as Drabinski emphasizes, highlight remnants that encourage ongoing dialogue and critical reflection.[50] And we must not downplay the civic implications of public institutions leveraging their social media and social privilege. When the Onondaga Free Library, outside Syracuse, shared about "Melissa's Story" on Instagram, the post's text not only endorsed the book but sent a clear message about the library's values: "We love #sharpieactivism Thanks Alex Gino for writing this beautiful book and for giving it its new perfect title!"[51]

"WHAT HAPPENED TO THIS BOOK?"

During the peak months of #SharpieActivism, I made note of social media posts shared by school librarians. One such annotator, in Florida, corrected the book and also taped a selection of Gino's apology to the cover alongside a QR code linked to their post about #SharpieActivism. I also read posts by school librarians from Georgia, Idaho, Illinois, Kentucky, Massachusetts, Minnesota, New York, Ohio, Oregon, Vermont, and Wisconsin, as well as Canada, England, Germany, Japan, and Scotland. Many of these posts displayed annotated books in classrooms or libraries, and a few included students. When we spoke, Gino stressed the social importance—and personal dissonance—associated with students' accessing *Melissa* in schools: "It is really weird to be not just accepted, but actively brought into upper elementary and junior high schools to show other people the exact me who I wasn't shown [as a student] and . . . to [now] make my life doing something I didn't experience." School librarians have been instrumental in making Melissa and her experience visible to students. And while these annotators didn't describe their contributions to #SharpieActivism as a queer intervention, what you will read are the dialogic remnants—the enduring re/marks—of public pedagogy that circulated activism and affirmation.

I was heartened to follow the few dozen posts by school librarians who participated in #SharpieActivism given sobering facts about students' awareness of and access to library texts featuring LGBTQIA+ topics, narratives, and characters. According to GLSEN's 2021 National School Climate Survey, the biennial survey of US students about the school experiences of LGBTQIA+ youth, "under half of students (42.8%) reported that they could find information about LGBTQ+-related issues in their school library."[52] Furthermore, only 30 percent of students said "they would be somewhat or very comfortable talking about LGBTQ+ issues" with a school librarian.[53] While some librarians celebrated *Melissa* online and in school, we cannot disregard the potential risks of social media attributed to individual justice-oriented advocacy. Today's book-banning efforts—which primarily target school libraries—are often complemented by weaponized social media, trolling, and the digital harassment of librarians, resulting in "an unprecedented wave of hostility."[54] Unlike public libraries that promoted

#SharpieActivism with posts from organizational accounts, similar acts of public pedagogy by school librarians are read as posts communicating educational and personal values. The stakes are different.[55] As such, I'm grateful for three librarians who entrusted me to share their practice so that we may appreciate annotation-as-activism in schools, as well as students' embrace of Melissa and her story.

In September of 2021, at the beginning of the new school year, Carolyn Bailey and her colleagues at Princeton Middle School, in New Jersey, invited students to join #SharpieActivism through a collaborative after-school activity. The school's event was advertised with two clear instructions: "Help us fix all the copies of Melissa's Story by Alex Gino that we can find," and "Bring your own copy, or have a chance to win one."[56] During the event, Bailey and colleagues facilitated students' book-marking through the creation of annotated covers. They also updated a centuries-old annotation artifact to further augment the group's #SharpieActivism. Each student received a large shipping label, custom-printed with an elaborate design, that was then affixed inside the cover of each corrected book. Bailey and colleagues had created #SharpieActivism bookplates. This familiar form of annotation, often indicating a mark of book ownership, instead functioned as a re/mark that asked: "What Happened To This Book?" The bookplate quoted and visually glossed Gino's blog post, with words underlined and circled ("fix the title yourself"), included a QR code linked to Gino's post, and also highlighted the hashtag. #SharpieActivism by Bailey and colleagues was meaningful for various reasons—they dedicated space and time for students to learn (more) about the book, explained the purpose of annotation, guided students to mark book covers in a supportive social environment, and paired students' aesthetic creativity with the library's descriptive bookplate.

That same month, a school librarian in British Columbia creatively remixed another physical attribute of library books to further guide students' engagement with #SharpieActivism. Christopher Hunt, an elementary school teacher-librarian, created two copies of Melissa with interior pocket envelopes repurposed for a new cause; what once held stamped circulation cards now prompted student inquiry. Hunt added a handwritten message to the "Date Due" pockets: "This book used to have a different title and cover. Read about why Mr. Hunt changed it." Folded and placed inside

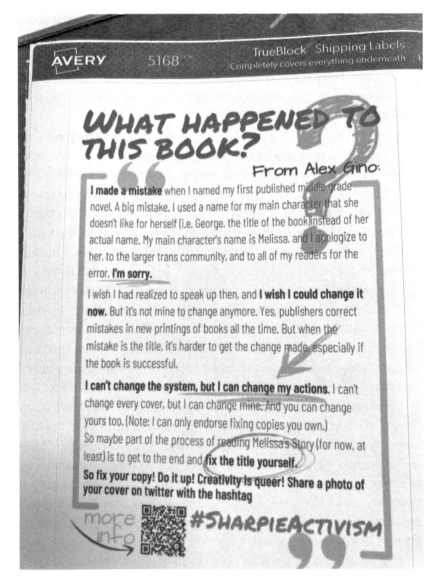

5.8 A #SharpieActivism shipping label-turned-bookplate used by middle school students to mark annotated copies of *Melissa*. Courtesy of Carolyn Bailey.

5.9 Annotated copies of *Melissa* created for a school library. Courtesy of Christopher Hunt/@ExLibrisMrHunt.

each pocket envelop was a printed copy of Gino's blog post, marked with Hunt's marginalia playfully requesting: "Return me to the pocket in Melissa's Story." Hunt's students were "quite intrigued" by the annotated books, he told me, especially after he "booktalked" the new title and showed other #SharpieActivism examples: "Some kids were doubly interested to borrow the book and read the information in more detail. It added a layer of excitement to reading a story about a trans kid, even if the student in question would already have borrowed the unaltered book."[57] Beyond his library and students, Hunt was forthcoming about #SharpieActivism as a "teachable moment" whereby routine librarianship became justice-aligned public pedagogy: "It was a chance to effect human rights changes for transgender people in real time by adding visible support (especially if shared online) and putting pressure on a company to do the right thing. It beautifully illustrated how, once somebody is transitioning, and you now know their real, proper gender and name, you need to respect it and use it. It's not their preference—it's their proper self, and it's their right, so it's up to you to change in accordance." Hunt's only regret, in retrospect, was that students didn't join him as annotators when marking the school's two copies of *Melissa*. Should a similar circumstance occur in the future, with authors who "would prefer their older works reflect their new and proper names," Hunt contemplated, "I'd have students who were interested do the annotations."

A few months after Bailey and Hunt shared their annotated copies of *Melissa*, I was contacted by a school librarian who wished to publicly— and anonymously—share a different type of #SharpieActivism story. This school librarian requested my assistance publicizing her experience because #SharpieActivism resulted in attempted censorship and contributed to her departure from a middle school where she had served for more than a decade. We eventually published her account as a blog post for We Need Diverse Books, the nonprofit organization that advocates for greater diversity in the publishing industry, as an example of how school librarians can resist the censorship of LGBTQIA+ books.[58] Briefly, this librarian invited students with her school's Gay-Straight Alliance Affinity Group to annotate the library's single copy of *Melissa*. The students did so collaboratively, creating "a beautiful and thoughtful cover that validated names, pronouns, and representation." Additionally, students wrote a short statement about why they corrected the cover and, similar to Bailey's bookplate and Hunt's pocket envelop, pasted this re/mark inside the book so that readers had easy access to contextual information about the change. The librarian then presented about #SharpieActivism and shared the students' annotated book at the school's weekly assembly during time reserved for library announcements. Following that announcement, the librarian received an email from a parent who "expressed concerns I had promoted a banned book. They took issue with Melissa's trans identity because they wanted to talk with their child about 'sensitive content.' At the time, four students and one faculty member publicly identified as trans. Claiming *Melissa* featured sensitive content, and therefore should be removed, was dangerous and hurtful." School representatives met with the parent, defended the librarian's decisions, and ensured students would continue accessing and reading *Melissa*. Nonetheless, the incident further eroded trust among the school's broader community, especially given "pushback about LGBTQ+ content in the past," and highlighted a lack of proactive support for library resources that represented LGBTQIA+ experiences. "The complexities of this incident are at the crux of educators' exhaustion and fear," this school librarian shared with me. "How do we acknowledge concern while also fiercely advocating for LGBTQ+ students and faculty?"

Libraries mark books for various functional reasons; we now know libraries can also annotate books with re/marks about trans pride and justice. Librarians uplifted Alex Gino's call for #SharpieActivism in what became—over many months and among both public and school libraries—a collective queer intervention acknowledging the contingency of how a book is named, organized, and accessed. Carolyn Bailey, Christopher Hunt, the anonymous educator who resisted book censorship, and other librarians who celebrated *Melissa* all understood how the discerning placement of marks on physical objects could productively influence dialogue about social belonging. The annotation of #SharpieActivism among the "quotidian aspects" of librarianship provided publics, including children at schools and libraries, with critical book marks. Annotated book covers and updated library catalogs demonstrated how people accept change, resist harmful ideology, and envision more hopeful futures. Librarians' creative book marks featured an amalgam of paper, markers, tape, labels, stickers, pockets, QR codes, videos, and hashtags. These hybrid compositions revealed contrasting tension across covers where the rightful presence of "Melissa's Story" outshined the still-visible traces of rejected "George." And librarians also gifted us with civic book marks that expanded what we may expect from libraries in a society beset by partisan censorship. Libraries are civic spaces where the power of language can center a trans protagonist, promote #transpride, and curate texts that dignify LGBTQIA+ narratives. While *Melissa* was the first book transformed by #SharpieActivism, I doubt it will be the last. Similar re/marks will flourish the next time annotators, including librarians, wield their markers in solidarity and deface books as a sign of respect.

6

MA(R)KING NARRATIVES

We are annotators whose re/marks can compose more just narratives and futures.

Like Harriet Tubman, who did so with "her mark" written decades after the Civil War, alongside those who endorsed her acts of literacy and advocacy. Lizbeth De La Cruz Santana did so, too, at Playas de Tijuana, accompanied by a community of *rascuache* artists whose stories transcend boundaries. As did nine-year-old Abigail Matthews in New Orleans, as she and her third-grade peers reimagined their city's memorial landscape. And Alex Gino did so with their book, inspiring handwritten titles of respect and viral social activism. Annotators of conscience have acted, in concert and in diverse contexts, to substantiate the societal relevance and political utility of annotation. Yes, let us encourage readers to write private marginalia in their books. And yes, students should annotate as a reading comprehension strategy in schools. Yet there is more to this ubiquitous and enduring literacy practice. With this book, I committed to honor the actions of annotators, whether eminent or anonymous, and to elevate how their material re/marks mediated justice-centered possibility. We now know that is attainable.

I have demonstrated how the social life of re/marks eclipses the conventional forms and reductive purposes of annotation, for these participatory traces are a means by which people write historical memory, resist harmful ideology, and broadcast solidarity and social change. Across four cases, I sought out and analyzed an original category of annotation—as located in archives and libraries, on walls and books, atop maps and monuments, and along byways and all manner of margins—to detail how such notes advance counternarratives and envision justice-directed social futures. This book is a study of how common marks make consequential narratives about land and legacy, memory and identity. And the aim of this concluding chapter is twofold: first, I will present a new conceptual perspective toward annotation scholarship that emphasizes the critical, syncretic, and civic qualities we witnessed in prior chapters; and second, I'll provide you with some practical guidance about how to recognize, read, and write your own re/marks. In service of both objectives, I will continue to share examples from my research that explicate common themes among our cases and help demark this latent promise of annotation.

Here, for instance, is one compelling set of notes—differing in material form and literary conviction from what's typically identified as annotation—that informs my refreshed understanding of how annotators can memorialize movement across boundaries, contribute personal reverence to civic narratives, and honor the pursuit of justice.

Across the US, approximately two dozen public monuments honor Harriet Tubman.[1] Only one statue is located at a courthouse. Dedicated in September 2022, Beacon of Hope is a large bronze monument that stands outside the Dorchester County Courthouse in Cambridge, Maryland, just a handful of miles from her birthplace.[2] A monument to Tubman at a courthouse is an anomaly of the American memorial landscape. According to *Whose Heritage?* data compiled by the Southern Poverty Law Center, 301 monuments to the Confederacy remain standing, as of January 2024, on courthouse grounds in fifteen states.[3] As constitutional law scholar Roger Hartley writes, "when the location of a Confederate monument is a courthouse lawn, that location symbolically implies that the courthouse does not represent justice for all."[4] Concern about a monument's location and symbolism reminds us that it is useful to read social texts in political contexts. In chapter 4, we read how America's memorial landscape is inscribed with white supremacist ideology and also how annotators' efforts have resisted and reimagined the vestiges of hatred in public memory. I visited Beacon of Hope two weeks after its dedication during my travels along

6.1 The Harriet Tubman Beacon of Hope monument at Dorchester County Courthouse in Cambridge, Maryland, with engraved brick path. Photograph by author (2022).

the Tubman Byway, related in chapter 2. The statue is an evocative composition of Tubman offering a key to a shackled representation of her younger self. The monument is also annotated with 243 engraved bricks. And these markers of place and purpose are aligned, beside Tubman, as a path oriented north.

To read "By Any Means Necessary" on a brick added to Tubman's Beacon of Hope monument invites comprehension of how, at this site of historical injustices, marks make visible ground truths and testimonials. It was at this courthouse, in 1850, that Tubman's niece Kessiah Jolley Bowley and her children, James Alfred and baby Araminta, escaped the auction block. That December, while in Philadelphia, Tubman received word that her niece was to be auctioned. Tubman promptly traveled back across the Mason–Dixon line to Baltimore and communicated with Kessiah's husband, John Bowley, who was manumitted in the 1840s and worked as a shipbuilder and blacksmith in Cambridge. Together, Tubman and Bowley "devised a scheme to spirit Kessiah and her two children away."[5] During the auction, Bowley surreptitiously secured the highest bid for Kessiah without revealing his identity. Prior to payment, however, he managed to move Kessiah and their children into hiding; that evening, they traveled by boat to Baltimore and "found safety with Tubman" who then guided their self-emancipation through Philadelphia.[6] The Bowleys were the first of approximately seventy to eighty individuals who liberated themselves with Tubman's assistance during at least thirteen trips over the next decade. At the courthouse, I didn't skim the bricks only as a list of monument benefactors, though many do name local families, businesses, and civic organizations that helped fund this memorial. Rather, I read these re/ marks as a curated testament of reclamation, for a public setting once witness to the administration of chattel slavery can counternarrate stories of resilience and human dignity.

Beacon of Hope has rewritten the memorial landscape in Dorchester County. And the inscribed bricks accompanying the monument neither redact nor revise history. A few bricks establish intertextuality between the monument and the Bible, appropriate given Tubman's faith, as with Romans 15:1: "We Who Are Strong Ought To Bear With The Frailties Of The Weak And Not To Please Ourselves." About a dozen bricks address

Tubman's legacy of justice: "Struggle Continues," "Working 4 Justice In The Spirit of Harriet," "A Life Lived For Liberty & Justice," "Solidarity," "I Am The Blade Which Can Not Be Broken," and "May Her Courage Lift Our Hearts & Inspire Our Deeds!" One brick reinterprets a contemporary expression to comment on Tubman's historic role in emancipation across boundaries: "Nevertheless She Persisted." Two hundred and forty-three bricks landmark the Bowley's pathway to liberation. It's implausible that Beacon of Hope viewers are not also brick readers. As re/marks on power, these notes help restore—and restory—knowledge about Tubman, her family, and the means necessary to achieve justice.

REFRAMING MY RE/MARKS

From a statue on the Eastern Shore to murals painting the Pacific coast, my travels also brought me into contact with methods and ideas previously distanced from the scholarship of annotation. "Opening Remarks" noted how the social life of annotation transcends literary studies of book readership, as well as educational research about student performance, for this literacy practice has added to the layered palimpsests of our natural and cultural environments. Accordingly, my exploratory survey of re/marks benefitted from interdisciplinarity, as I embraced art history and human geography, and prior studies of cartography and classification, among other topics. My eclectic stance meant that I read more than book marginalia to enliven the impressions and locations of annotation that we can now call re/marks. I found it instructive to read collections of notes, often authored by groups of annotators whose traces spanned settings and time, to discern influential messages. And, as with the engraved bricks added to Beacon of Hope, I read these annotations within social and historical contexts as literacy acts that both disputed and expressed power. In light of our cases, how do I now comprehend the defining qualities of re/marks, whether such notes are added to documents or monuments, walls or books?

I began my research aware of annotation as a ubiquitous literacy practice that appears across surfaces and settings. It is my hope that we acknowledge re/marks as a type of annotation entangled with texts textured by power. While we saw, quite clearly, individuals with ascribed bureaucratic

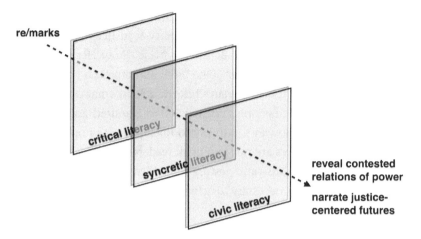

6.2 A conceptual perspective to perceive re/marks on power and justice.

and cultural authority inscribe their priorities and ideologies onto various texts, we also observed the disruptive power of annotators who rejected iconography, created art, honored community, and circulated activism. In a return to my disciplinary terrain, I am keen to consider how three complementary developments in literacy studies—albeit stances not often applied to acts of annotation—are relevant to the notes we encountered. Specifically, I broaden my lens to reframe the vitality of re/marks amid respected understandings of critical, syncretic, and civic literacy. Given prior evidence, I assert that a new conceptual perspective toward annotation can reveal contested relations of power and narrate justice-centered futures.

While writing this book, three interdependent literacy concepts surfaced as timely and relevant to my study of re/marks. Scholars, across eras and traditions, have championed various ideas to explain the literary merits and educational benefits of annotation. Today, re/marks are (re)writing our world with annotators' commentary on authority and justice. It is my conclusion that future analyses will be insightful when these public traces are intentionally perceived as critical, syncretic, and civic literacy. And I am optimistic that a novel conceptual perspective—represented in figure 6.2—can guide new chapters of inquiry about notes remarking on power.

RE/MARKS ARE CRITICAL

The re/marks that we read should be perceived as *critical literacy*. Critical literacies comprise practices and dispositions that enable people within their everyday contexts to recognize discourses of power, interrogate bias in media, and critique dominant authority. As literacy theorist Allan Luke writes, critical literacy "refers to use of the technologies of print and other media of communication to analyze, critique, and transform the norms, rule systems, and practices governing the social fields of everyday life."[7] For decades, scholars and educators have identified various theoretical traditions and pedagogical expressions associated with critical literacies, while also recognizing that an embrace of criticality eschews singular definition and demands reflexivity about agency and ideology.[8] Nonetheless, one tenet of critical literacies is the synthesis of textual analysis with contextual awareness, oftentimes associated with educator Paulo Freire's dialogic methods and advocacy for critical consciousness.[9] Scholar Donald Macedo, who collaborated with Freire, wrote three decades ago that critical literacy demands mutual comprehension of words and the world: "We must first read the world—the cultural, social, and political practices that constitute it—before we can make sense of the word-level description of reality."[10] Each of our prior chapters began by reading the world so as to scrutinize legible "word-level" annotations of dominant ideology that augmented primary source texts.

In the case of Harriet Tubman's military service, concern for critical literacy influenced my description of fourteen annotations added to her Civil War pension file between 1890 and 1895 that exhibited bureaucratic assessment and corroborated racial discrimination in the pension system. I also suggested that the marginal note added to Tubman's 1899 Widow's Pension form—stating "Claimant pensioned as Harriet Davis widow of Nelson Davis alias Nelson Charles"—be critiqued because of patriarchal cultural norms and partisan conciliation that erased Tubman's "double claim" to her pension. When studying the marked boundary between Mexico and the US, I examined how, in 1848, the "Boundary Line Linea Divisoria" was ruled atop an imprecisely traced reproduction of Don Juan Pantoja's 1782 Plano del Puerto de San Diego map, inscribed with notes of conquest, and then added to the Treaty of Guadalupe Hidalgo. The plenipotentiaries who signed and sealed this treaty were annotators—as was US Army Captain Robert E. Lee, who most certainly had a hand in making and marking this authenticated map that delimited a divisive border. In chapter 4, our survey of the American memorial landscape began at the University of North Carolina at Chapel Hill where a Confederate monument known as Silent Sam stood for 105 years. The statue's 1913 dedication is well-known for blatantly celebrating white supremacy and racial violence, yet I focused our attention on an overlooked annotation in the speech of a Klan member who lauded university students for sacrificing their "precious blood" on behalf of the Confederacy. And, in the previous chapter, I reviewed how heteronormative classification practices have marked library books with call numbers that are offensive to LGBTQIA+ communities. Hegemonic book marks are the result of nineteenth-century classification schemes, like the Dewey Decimal Classification system, and despite ongoing correction illustrate the inherently problematic act of classifying—and then annotating with call numbers—books about gender and sexuality. Across cases, my critical reading of the world allowed me to subsequently chronicle how re/marks emerged from inscriptions of injustice.

We also saw annotators respond to inequities with re/marks of resistance and creativity, thereby demonstrating how critical literacies "afford the ability to produce powerful texts that address injustices in our lived worlds."[11] Harriet Tubman was an annotator. Tubman's handwritten X marked nine documents between 1890 and 1898 while she petitioned the US government for her rightful pension and "her mark" was an act of critical literacy that recorded a steadfast fight for justice. At Playas de Tijuana, we viewed murals by scholar De La Cruz Santana, military veterans Alex Murillo and Amos Gregory, and artist Enrique Chiu—all annotators—whose public art contradicts presumed authority by honoring human dignity. The Playas de Tijuana Mural Project, the Deported Veterans Mural Project, and Mural de la Hermandad exemplify what architect Teddy Cruz describes as the potential of "transforming public space into an experimental platform to research new forms of knowledge, pedagogy, and public participation, whose point of departure is the visualization of environmental and political conflict."[12] In "Marked Men," we appraised the figurative highlighting of controversial monuments by many annotators, including: Maya Little, who added "historical context" to Silent Sam with her blood and red ink; The

Kudzu Project craftivists, who yarn bombed Confederate statues throughout Virginia after the 2017 white nationalist rally in Charlottesville; and Reclaiming the Monument projectionists, who highlighted the Robert E. Lee Monument in Richmond throughout the summer of 2020. We also learned from educator Amy Dickerson and her class of third-grade students in New Orleans whose self-published book *Courageous, Eccentric, Diverse* illustrated an alternative memorial landscape following the 2017 removal of four Confederate monuments. As for #SharpieActivism, the campaign succeeded because author Gino modeled the ease and necessity of marking *Melissa* as transgender justice. I further argued that public and school librarians, like Carolyn Bailey and Christopher Hunt, circulated "Melissa's Story" because shared book marks were a queer intervention remarking on trans pride and affirming LGBTQIA+ narratives. I presented four justice-centered analyses of annotators' public statements, each case shaped by critique and creativity, to establish how reading annotation as critical literacy reveals the power of re/marks.

RE/MARKS ARE SYNCRETIC

"Annotation," Courtney McClellan informed me while writing this book, "is a gesture of care."[13] McClellan is an artist, former collaborator, and annotator.[14] In our conversation, she also emphasized that annotations have "the capacity to hold paradoxes." Admittedly, it may seem contradictory for me to discuss how re/marks demonstrate critical literacy and to then observe how annotation is also valued as a gesture of care. The incongruity of notes that hold critique and care—the inherent hybridity of marks which jointly interrupt injustice and inspire change—can be usefully explained if we further recognize this form of annotation as *syncretic literacy*.

Syncretism is a second literacy concept that illuminates the often paradoxical—and powerful—complexities of re/marks detailed in our prior chapters. My interest in syncretic literacy is principally influenced by the work of professor Kris Gutiérrez whose scholarship has demonstrated that "syncretic learning reorganizes everyday and school-based literacy practices and can help support the development of powerful literacies that challenge current models of academic literacy."[15] For Gutiérrez and her colleagues, syncretism is a strategic fusion of oppositional perspectives and hybrid practices, transgressing boundaries, time, and marginal spaces not often "sanctioned as educational."[16] From this stance, the syncretism of annotator literacy is evident in a social practice as germane to learners' school grades as it is to their street graffiti. More specifically, we saw how re/marks functioned to unify reading with writing, couple individual cognition with social activism, and blur the singular author with multivocal authority. Pertinent to our cases, Gutiérrez's approach to syncretism is also historically rooted: "By attending to historicity, individual practices are connected to their cultural and historical context . . . In this way, literacy practices are not discretely circumscribed phenomena but instead occur as a part of laminated, overlapping, and interwoven social phenomena across time and space."[17] Whether with the laminated "History Under Construction" signage at Muir Woods National Monument or Beacon of Hope and its bricks, historical re/marks are woven into our critical reading and writing of everyday texts, settings, and social phenomena. Re/marks both contest and create narratives and whether such notes are idiosyncratic or ordinary; as McClellan reminded me, annotations "hold clarity and messiness simultaneously," complementing both "scholarly but also incredibly colloquial contexts."

During my research, I read a set of notes along the US–Mexico border that literally and figuratively symbolized how re/marks can function as a gesture of care holding paradox. There was a section of Mural de la Hermandad at Playas de Tijuana that featured the caring marks of children. Away from the Malecón and beach surf, near overgrown garden beds and concrete benches, about a dozen slats of the former border wall displayed sincere beauty amid imposing indignity. When I visited, just months before this section of the barrier was razed and replaced, I immediately noticed the handprints. Most were small and recognizable as those belonging to children—not much larger than the hands of my four-year-old son—in red, orange, blue, pink, yellow, and green, some smudged, a few faded. Two hands were outlined with black marker, presumably added sometime after the painted handprints, the literal traces of presence. Children stood here. They imprinted care; tender touches on a wall of death. Children annotated power with morality. Seven slats also displayed brief messages: "Paz y Amor," "Solo Por Hoy / Se Feliz," "Aquí Ahora," and "Voco." "Incansables"

6.3 Section of Mural de la Hermandad at Playas de Tijuana (this wall section was subsequently removed). Photograph by author (2023).

appeared next to the faded note "Be Happy." A small purple mariposa, the conspicuous symbol of migration, was painted near the ground, one among many decorating the wall. Among the few English words written along this section of the mural was "Just Love." How was I to interpret the paradoxical connotations of "just"—as personal imperative or political indictment? This physical manifestation of inhumane ideology, a barrier which neither advances nor represents justice, was marked by anonymous annotators whose gestures cared for future readers. Glaring contradictions of an unnatural boundary were distilled in the humble handprint of a child.

The re/marks that I saw at Playas de Tijuana were syncretic. Now, these notes are both a memory and harbinger—for children will stand before today's taller and more aggressive border wall, touch this injustice with their hands, and leave new traces of "Paz y Amor" that care for a better tomorrow. We reached similar conclusions when reading about children who authored *Courageous, Eccentric, Diverse* and those who joined #SharpieActivism. Re/marks are best explained as a syncretic literacy, for this conceptual commitment directs our analysis to contradictions among text, context, and emergent interpretation.

RE/MARKS ARE CIVIC

Just as syncretism is an idea compatible with critical literacy, so, too, is a critical reading and writing of the world "inextricably linked with civic participation."[18] Every case in this book documented the ways in which mark-makers made sense of public discourses, joined social movements of varying scale and configuration, and then addressed common concerns with annotation; in other words, annotators' literacy acts were expressly civic. My third and final proposition is that we also perceive re/marks as a *civic literacy*.

For many years, traditional civic engagement in the US has emphasized familiarity with existing governance processes, community volunteerism, media consumption, and formal activities like voting. Yet these customary civic efforts often fail to reflect—much less pragmatically alter—the lived experiences of nondominant individuals, especially youth, as well as the aspirations of groups accorded less privilege and power. There is an acute need for "critically relevant civics,"[19] as acknowledged by both social scientists and literacy scholars, that can encourage learners' sociopolitical development and action.[20] My knowledge of civic literacy as justice-centered action draws from the work of education professors Nicole Mirra and Antero Garcia; their scholarship advocates new models of civic imagination as consonant with political resistance and creative meaning-making for "radically reorienting the nature and purpose of shared democratic life toward equity, empathy, and justice."[21] I find particularly useful Mirra and Garcia's attention to civic *composing* practices that can span settings and foster civic innovation.[22] As a synthesis of reading, writing, and multimodal production, civic composing includes practices of dialogue, persuasion, solidarity, and action, as well as compositions that produce counternarratives since "writing against is a form of civic literacy that manifests new realities."[23] Particularly when re/marks mediate public expression—as with stamped banknotes, the figurative highlighting of problematic monuments, and hashtags affirming LGBTQIA+ youth—outcomes may consist of civic compositions that write against a wrong and imagine new counternarratives.

6.4 Hostile Terrain 94 wall map installed at the Museum of Us in San Diego. Photograph by author (2023).

How does a civic composition form and in what ways might re/marks augment such a text? While conducting research in San Diego, I stood before a literal and solemn memorial landscape comprised of notes unambiguously critical, syncretic, and civic. The re/marks feature people's names—as handwritten gestures of care—and repurposed a bureaucratic marker of death to respectfully identify and repeatedly commemorate ancestors.

In 1994, the US Border Patrol began Prevention Through Deterrence (PTD), a strategy to discourage undocumented migrants from crossing the US–Mexico border in and around urban ports of entry. When the Border Patrol first proposed PTD, it predicted that "with traditional entry and smuggling routes disrupted, illegal traffic will be deterred, or forced over more hostile terrain, less suited for crossing and more suited for enforcement."[24] That "hostile terrain" was the desert. This strategy presumed that migrants would cross the border on foot, in remote areas, where the natural environment functioned as a physical deterrent to movement. In *The Land of Open Graves*, anthropologist Jason De León reviews how PTD policy contributed to migrant deaths along the border, as "the correlation between the funneling of people toward desolate regions of the border and an upsurge in fatalities is strong." De León's assessment of PTD is candid: "Rather than shooting people as they jumped the fence, Prevention Through Deterrence set the stage for the desert to become the new 'victimizer' of border transgressors."[25] By one US government estimate, over eight thousand migrants have died along the border since the late 1990s, mostly from exposure and dehydration; the number is likely far higher, for De León acknowledges "the actual number of people who lose their lives while migrating will forever remain unknown."[26] Complementing his scholarship, De León is director of the nonprofit Undocumented Migration Project that has critiqued PTD by organizing the participatory art installation Hostile Terrain 94 (HT94). In San Diego, I had an opportunity to view HT94 and its annotated map, marked with thousands of names, that memorializes individuals who died crossing hostile terrain.

Since 2019, approximately one hundred hosting partners around the world, mostly at universities, have exhibited HT94 using the project's accessible materials and participatory installation process. Each partner receives a map of the Sonoran Desert in Southern Arizona and thousands of toe tags to identify people. Volunteers at each site consult data from the Pima County Office of the Medical Examiner and the nonprofit organization Humane Borders to inscribe tags that are then attached to the map.[27] The version of HT94 that I read at San Diego's Museum of Us opened in 2021 with 3,205 toe tags—all re/marks—representing someone who died crossing the Sonoran Desert between the mid-1990s and 2020. Subsequent iterations of HT94 display over 3,800 tags based on data compiled through 2022. Most of the tags are manila as that color represents an identified person—their name is written on the tag. Orange tags represent unknown human remains labeled "unidentified." Other information on the tags includes the person's age, sex, cause of death, body condition, and the latitude and longitude where they were found. HT94 describes the map as a memorial "co-constructed by local volunteers. Each tag is hand-written by community members as a humble way to honor the dead, people who are now ancestors. The physical act of writing out their names and information invites participants to reflect, witness, and stand in solidarity with those who have lost their lives in search of a better one. The tags are placed

6.5 Hostile Terrain 94 toe tags, with the re/mark "you are not forgotten" partially visible. Photograph by author (2023).

in the exact location where the person's remains were found in the desert."[28] Over the past few years, hundreds of anonymous HT94 annotators have collectively written approximately 300,000 tags.

In a 2020 article about HT94, De León discussed the importance of volunteers, often university students, writing the toe tags by hand. "I wanted to put names to the dead," he said. "This is an act of witnessing. The data come from a Microsoft database. We're asking volunteers to breathe life into the data by writing out the details. That was the closest way we could think of to get someone to feel the human cost. I've filled out hundreds of toe tags. It doesn't get any easier."[29] Writing tags was challenging for one museum staff member-turned-HT94 volunteer who spoke with me during my visit. He described the writing process as full of "strong moments, especially when their age," he paused. "You know, for the young kids." I recalled one manila tag identifying a two-year-old girl. I then asked about another detail, for I noticed "you are" added to the blank back of one orange tag (left side of figure 6.5). Did volunteers write comments on the back of some tags? He confirmed they had. I returned to the memorial and touched it slowly, carefully, glimpsing that tag's additional re/mark. A volunteer wrote, "you are not forgotten."

As I subsequently learned, "volunteers who fill out tags are welcome to write a personal message on the backs of the tags."[30] HT94 invites volunteers to process grief with handwritten annotations that endure as traces of commemoration. During installation at the University of Michigan, for instance, student volunteers annotated tags with: "Just a child;" "May her memory be for a blessing;" "I will remember;" and "Este año voy a cumplir 20 años. Voy a vivir mi vida recordando que soy bendecida. Descansa en Paz."[31] Similar re/marks were added by students at Pennsylvania State University: "You are remembered. I am sorry your life was not protected & valued by my country. I will fight for change;" "the desert erases people;" "Josefina, we bear witness;" "Cosme, you are not forgotten;" and "Your life and death have meaning. You are missed."[32] And after a faculty workshop at Cabrillo College, in California, volunteers annotated tags with the phrases: "Descansa en paz | con los angeles | fuiste uno;" and "Nunca te voya olvidar. Los nombres saben Dios."[33] With a growing number of installations—each distinct because of continuing personal tragedy on the border and volunteers' notes on wall maps—HT94 publicizes a critical, syncretic, and civic narrative composed by annotators who write against injustice with re/marks of solidarity.

INSCRIBING YOUR RE/MARKS

The remarkable potential of annotation can be amplified when we engage this practice as a critical, syncretic, and civic literacy. Furthermore, you can help bring re/marks into dialogue with the political realities of education, as well as society writ large. In response to unjust traces, groups of annotators have made public re/marks of resistance and creativity, often with simple tools and accessible methods, thereby altering familiar texts and aligning everyday contexts toward more just social futures. We learned that De La Cruz Santana read "ten years" written on the Mexican side of the border wall, researched the meaning of migration bars, and referenced this message when explaining to me how she curated the Playas de Tijuana Mural Project. She annotated among an emergent collective of artists. We heard how third-grader Abigail Matthews read the Solomon Northup place marker near her school in the French Quarter, recognized the inequity between a small sign and standing Confederate statues, and reimagined New Orleans' memorial landscape with a monument to Northup. She annotated alongside her classmates. How, as an annotator, might you notice and then compose annotation that is critical, syncretic, and civic? I conclude with four practical recommendations, each mutually represented by a final example from my research.

First, seek out contested symbols and spaces for such contexts often exhibit re/marks. Granted, you may already move across material and ideological margins, recognizing disputed texts and attendant notes as familiar land-marks. And no, you need not cross guarded borders or conduct archival research to situate yourself amid contested (con)texts. As I modeled, you can follow the record of scholars attuned to systemic challenges and principled resistance. Our review of efforts to place Harriet Tubman's portrait on the $20 banknote spotlighted historian Clarence Lusane's assessment that America's "contested territory" includes currency, iconography, public memorials, and geographical place names. In "Marking Boundaries," I approached the historic limit between Upper and Lower California—today's border separating San Diego from Tijuana—neither as neutral nor a given; rather, it's a marge, or what historian John Stilgoe calls a zone "contested by wilderness and human order."[34] Chapter 4 emphasized the social construction of historical memory, as I foregrounded scholar Elizabeth Alexander's critique in the *National Monument Audit* that memorials are problematic precisely because they can misrepresent history and erase the contributions of nondominant groups. And in "Book Marks," our case reviewed library classification and featured scholar Melissa Adler's research about the bias of authoritative categories, as with the Library of Congress Classification subclass HQ, that we then read as "a highly contested space."[35] Re/marks evidence annotators responding to problematic surroundings and dominant discourses. While reading your worlds, where might this form of annotation aid comprehension of controversial symbols and spaces?

Second, observe how re/marks expose counternarratives concealed amid everyday texts. In their book *Redaction*, artist Titus Kaphar and poet Reginald Dwayne Betts exhibit redacted civil rights lawsuits with discernment and empathy, revealing disregarded injustices of American carcerality and the indignities of state-sanctioned oppression.[36] What could be construed as so-called blackout poetry is, in my reading, a harrowing use of re/marks to recompose obscured truths, illustrating scholar Shannon Mattern's analysis that "redaction can serve diverse ethical and political ends, and it even contains a latent capacity for redemption: it can be reparative and generative even as it flags destructive practices."[37] We experienced similar illuminating effects in each of our cases as re/marks revealed offenses and wrote justice-directed statements. Twenty-five place markers along the Tubman Byway in Maryland stand as a visible intervention countering the erasure of Black resistance and liberation. Dozens of people were named in the Deported Veterans Mural Project, each individual signaling obscured policy reforms and bureaucratic hurdles that continue afflicting deported US veterans and their families.[38] The hashtags, names, graffiti, and splattered paint that highlighted white supremacist monuments made explicit missing "historical context" that both student Maya Little and historian Karen Cox knew was long absent from Confederate memorials. And the partial redaction of "George" on book covers invigorated "Melissa's Story" and counternarrated how identity and affirmation change over time. What unwritten message may be uncovered and broadcast by your re/marks?

Third, compose your re/marks with simple and accessible tools. Annotation has endured for centuries as a familiar literacy practice because objects that make marks atop texts are often inexpensive, easy to find, simple to use, and readily shared. Markers—the handheld kind, with ink and a cap—were used by annotators in all four cases: I was greeted by a bicentennial birthday card, and three colorful Sharpies, at the Harriet Tubman Underground Railroad State Park and Visitor Center; De La Cruz Santana and her collaborators used Sharpies to outline the Playas de Tijuana Mural Project's portraits onto cloth; I also used a Sharpie to write Gloria Anzaldúa's phrase "An Unnatural Boundary" onto the rusted border wall; the twenty-one student authors of *Courageous, Eccentric, Diverse* used markers (and crayons) to illustrate their proposed monuments; and, of course, #SharpieActivism. Stamps also left enduring traces, as with artist Dano Wall's Tubman Stamp, purchased over seven thousand times, the seals of plenipotentiaries added to the authenticated map of the Treaty of Guadalupe Hidalgo, and classification call numbers routinely stamped by librarians onto books. Paint created murals and highlighted monuments. Glue attached the Playas de Tijuana Mural Project's cloth strips onto the border wall's slats, affixed new covers and spine labels onto copies of *Melissa*, and collaged new monuments honoring Mahalia Jackson, Solomon Northup, and others onto photographs of abandoned pedestals. Even when more sophisticated technologies were used by annotators—as with Stoughton Public Library and Lyons Falls Library staff who posted #SharpieActivism TikTok videos—these tools broadened access to participatory literacies. Children, as learners in schools and libraries, easily and frequently use these objects to make their marks, too. Of the many tools in this book, what will you pick up to mediate your re/marks?

And fourth, appreciate how re/marks invite fellow annotators into a collaborative experience that galvanizes social change. In "Her Mark," we met Harriet Tubman's New York neighbors who, in 1898, petitioned the federal government to support her pension claim. And also Dave, at Kilgore Books, who helped me stamp my first Tubman twenty. These annotators, separated by nearly 125 years, facilitated public mark-making to redress circumstance and symbol. When I spoke with De La Cruz Santana about her group's efforts as *rascuache* artists, she mentioned how the mural's impermanence has motivated ongoing social and aesthetic commitments. "They [her collaborators] would send me messages like, 'Hey, Liz, this is happening, this is a photo of the mural, how it looks like right now,'" she told me, "'And we will touch [up] the blue paint or bring more glue, and we'll fix a face that's falling apart.' That for me became this idea of, people really cared about the border becoming something else, at least on the Mexican side." Many examples in "Marked Men" were the result of groups committed to a more inclusive memorial landscape. UNC students, like Little, had resisted and defaced Silent Sam for decades and they collectively brought it down; portraits projected onto the Lee Monument changed over weeks of protest in coordination with local activists; and *Courageous, Eccentric, Diverse* was published following class inquiry and collaboration with the local literacy organization 826 New Orleans. And part of Gino's brilliance was pairing their invitation to correct "Melissa's Story" with a hashtag that succinctly conveyed method and purpose. While most #SharpieActivism posts didn't go viral by typical measures, the campaign was broadly embraced and highly effective because Gino orchestrated annotation as a

6.6 History Lab installation at the San Diego History Center with sculptures *The Indian* and *The Padre* by Arthur Putnam. Photograph by author (2023).

participatory mark of respect for Melissa and "the larger trans community." How will your re/marks extend justice-centered efforts to rewrite notes and narratives?

I opened this book—and each chapter—stating a basic premise: You and I are annotators. If you doubted my sincerity, go seek out contested symbols and spaces, read new narratives unveiled by re/marks, consider adding your own with simple tools, and join with other mark-makers who are authoring social change. And here's another suggestion, too: You might just start with an X. Like I did, when I marked a work of art in a museum gallery.

As discussed in chapter 4, I'm skeptical of efforts to contextualize divisive monuments for such annotation is a pragmatic yet insufficient response to offensive public messages. While visiting the San Diego History Center, however, my doubt was momentarily tempered as I encountered hundreds of incisive, contradictory, and colorful sticky notes that exhibited young peoples' re/marks about two contested statues.

MA(R)KING NARRATIVES

In 2019, the city of San Diego and the San Diego History Center initiated a process to relocate sculptor Arthur Putnam's *The Indian* (completed in 1904) and *The Padre* (1908) from public display in Presidio Park. The sculptures were part of a series about California history commissioned in 1903 by newspaper publisher Edward W. Scripps; both were loaned to the History Center in 1933, became part of the collection in 1976, and then stood publicly in the park for decades. I found this History Lab installation in the very back of the center. A summary of the statues' provenance noted preservation and interpretation as reasons for the 2021 relocation. Now indoors, the statues are protected "from both climate and vandalism;" moreover, "critical context can be provided on the role of sculptures and monuments as artifacts that shed light on early 20th century ideas about 'progress,' 'race,' and 'civilization.'"[39] That "critical context" mentions *The Indian* is "a romanticized indigenous person from the Plains region," and that "the actual first people of this region, the Kumeyaay, were never acknowledged nor represented" by Putnam. As for *The Padre*, it is "often mistaken" for a depiction of Junípero Serra, though correspondence from Scripps refers to the sculpture as "Serra." Surrounded by sparse white walls and minimal signage, the bronze figures looked misplaced. I walked past them to an explosion of green, blue, yellow, orange, and pink sticky notes.

This participatory contextualization turned the far corner of a museum into a critical, syncretic, and civic learning environment. Questions in English and Spanish prompted visitors' responses: "What do you notice?" "How do you think these sculptures relate to San Diego's history?" "Do you think these sculptures represent history? How so?" The questions encouraged a careful reading of controversial symbols in current social contexts. Some of the sticky notes reflected a sophisticated understanding of colonialism, as with "Land Back No More Empty Words & Gestures!" and "colonial structures of power continue to harm POC communities." One aggressively defended the sculptures: "The statue was named 'The Indian' by the artist over 100 yrs ago. Just because you don't like it doesn't mean it should be updated. It's a part of history. Learn from it and move on—don't change it—change your perspective. Think better!" A few shared a conciliatory stance toward the value of preservation: "Preserve the statues, preserve the flags, preserve history (even bad history is history)." A child requested: "Please put the statues back in Presidio Park. We miss them." As a former literacy teacher, I noticed the writing of children and youth on most of the notes, likely added during class visits (the center prominently advertised its free educational programming). Young people remarked: "Do better," "Art is an expression of beauty," "It looks like he's praying," "I would love to see more statues of women," and "I think you should put more things about the Kumeyaay." Children asked: "What's on their minds when other people took their land?" and "What do these people have to do with San Diego?" Critical and syncretic literacies were evident among the public re/marks: "very amazing statues" appeared near "This is Native land."

I read the wall and selected a pink sticky note. To what question would I respond? And how might my re/mark complement the honesty and inquisitiveness of these young annotators? Alone in the quiet gallery, I recalled a conversation with scholar Debbie Reese about her annotation practices. In 2006, Reese founded American Indians in Children's Literature, a public resource which "provides critical analysis of Indigenous peoples in children's and young adult books."[40] Reese is an annotator. When she does not recommend educators teach a book featuring Indigenous peoples and topics, she will add a large red X over an image of the book's cover to quickly and unambiguously convey her assessment. Her annotated covers are then shared across social media and published on her website. "That red X conveys a lot of power," Reese told me. "I'm trying to use its power by attaching it to problematic books because teachers understand it right away."[41] Reese's strategy for "interrupting the image" of a controversial book motivates educators "to do the close read and analysis of it, because then they own that knowledge and they can apply it to other books." Inspired by Reese, I turned from the wall with my note in hand and applied an X on *The Indian* to temporarily interrupt its problematic messages.

I wonder what visitors noticed and how they responded. What re/marks would you have added and where would you stick a note?

REMARKABLE PROMISE

Annotation has been a common though sanctioned act for centuries, constrained as a marginal practice, often prohibited in physical objects, and considered largely irrelevant to social discourses. Alternatively, we know

MA(R)KING NARRATIVES   141

6.7 My sticky note with an X re/mark added to *The Indian*. Photograph by author (2023).

annotators can alter material conditions and political circumstances by inscribing words on the world and imprinting new images into awareness. Re/marks are a contemporary form and force of annotation that draw attention to long-standing struggles for power and justice. We are wise to look for, learn from, and make use of these notes.

I studied Harriet Tubman's pension file for days before noticing her mark. Without concern for annotation, I could have easily overlooked her handwritten X and remained unaware that evidence of her literacies persists on the pages of history. Re/marks elicit our attention, whether as an indicator of personal agency or as a record of political conquest. I scrutinized every version of Don Juan Pantoja's 1782 Plano del Puerto de San Diego that I could access—the original map archived at the Library of Congress, versions in nineteenth-century atlases, and the altered tracing added to the Treaty of Guadalupe Hidalgo—so as not to discount how subtle notes have mediated separation to this day. It is inconsiderate to dismiss annotation that scars a boundary, just as it is impractical to ignore a bronze statue splattered by blood. To examine the changing faces of America's memorial landscape, I did not disregard the actions of protestors resisting inherited symbols of racism and colonization. Whereas some may write off graffiti as disrespectful vandalism, I see annotators rewriting more just civic narratives. And as an educator, how could I not uplift the creative visions shared by children in *Courageous, Eccentric, Diverse*? Re/marks direct attention—when discovered in our archives and cities and when cultivated in our classrooms and libraries. And I analyzed #SharpieActivism as more than a moment to celebrate. To thoughtfully discuss mark-making in service of trans justice, I could not ignore heteronormativity written into the bibliographic classification practices of libraries. Throughout this book, I made deliberate choices about how to frame particular annotations as re/marks. And once read, there were transcendent notes—like Tubman's X and HT94 toe tags—that I couldn't forget. As you encounter annotation, both in books and the built environment, question whether you're reading a re/mark—and if so, I hope you heed its power.

I also demonstrated how to make sense of the re/marks we surveyed. I didn't prescribe a fixed method for textual analysis. Rather, I modeled how to meaningfully comprehend a distinct type of annotation that has rewritten our documents and discourses—and will continue to do so.

Complementing counternarratives in each case, I also offered an original conceptual perspective so literacy scholars and educators can better perceive how marks make narratives. As I suggested in "Opening Remarks," and as shown in prior chapters, annotation flourishes beyond book marginalia and individual reader response as this social activity catalyzes collective action against injustice. By positioning re/marks as critical literacy, we privileged how annotators used this practice to resist symbols of division and envision more just possibilities. We also benefitted by approaching re/marks as syncretic literacy, for annotators expressed clarity and contradiction in their notes, leaving us with traces of paradox. And our understanding of re/marks as civic literacy called attention to compositions of public conscience, as we witnessed annotators share narratives of remembrance, belonging, and admiration.

While reading page and place, you will determine how to comprehend the re/marks that you notice, question the problematic details of referent texts, and then respond given social and political contexts. *Re/Marks on Power* is an argument for adopting a new stance toward the steadfast composition and academic study of annotation predicated on commitments to critical, syncretic, and civic literacy. For I have no doubt that soon enough you will stumble across annotated books, banknotes, walls, boundaries, statues, signs, and social media. Perhaps you'll now consider how commonplace traces thoughtfully advance justice-centered narratives and futures. That is a mark of promise—and power—worthy of our attention, comprehension, and enduring authorship.

NOTES

CHAPTER 1

1. Andrew M. Stauffer, *Book Traces: Nineteenth-Century Readers and the Future of the Library* (Philadelphia: University of Pennsylvania Press, 2021), 6.

2. Robert Rubsam, "How Scribbling in the Margins Transformed My Reading," *New York Times Magazine*, November 2, 2021, https://www.nytimes.com/2021/11/02/magazine/take-notes-while-reading.html.

3. Courtney McClellan, "Chasing Things That Cannot Be Chased: Interview with Kameelah Janan Rasheed," *Art Papers*, accessed January 23, 2023, https://www.artpapers.org/chasing-the-things-that-cant-be-changed/.

4. Wendy Red Star, "Back to the Blanket: Wendy Red Star in Conversation with Josh T. Franco," in *Delegation* (New York: Aperture, 2022), 32.

5. Hope Corrigan, "On Instagram and TikTok, Annotating Books Is an Art," *Washington Post*, November 23, 2023, https://www.washingtonpost.com/books/2023/11/23/book-annotations/.

6. Jesse Morales-Small, "Annotate (A Lesson in Vengeance) with Me," YouTube Video, 15:07, November 1, 2021, https://youtu.be/6SaSGPABCeY.

7. MelReads, "How I Annotate My Books (Updated) Tips on Annotating for Beginners to Advanced Readers," YouTube Video, 21:06, December 5, 2021, https://youtu.be/ns-vCYVaybc.

8. H. J. Jackson, *Marginalia: Readers Writing in Books* (New Haven, CT: Yale University Press, 2001), 243.

9. American Library Association, "The State of America's Libraries 2022: A Report From the American Library Association," 2022, https://www.ala.org/news/sites/ala.org.news/files/content/state-of-americas-libraries-special-report-pandemic-year-two.pdf.

10. Remi Kalir and Antero Garcia, *Annotation* (Cambridge, MA: MIT Press, 2021).

11. My use of "land-marks" is intended to make visible the act of altering everyday places. To land-mark emphasizes activity (as with a verb), in contrast to my more conventional use of landmarks (as a noun), which refers to distinctive features of place.

12. Maha Bali, Ashley Boyd, and Remi Kalir, "Collaborative Reading and Writing," *Research in the Teaching of English* 57, no. 2 (November 2022): 200; see also my curated series of blog posts and resources about syllabus annotation at https://remikalir.com /annotatedsyllabus/.

13. Jeremiah Kalir, "'Annotation Is First Draft Thinking': Educators' Marginal Notes as Brave Writing, *English Journal* 110, no. 2 (2020): 62–68.

14. Ashley Harrell, "Muir Woods Park Staff Annotates Own Signs with Historical Corrections for Racism, Misogyny," *SFGATE*, August 26, 2021, https://www.sfgate.com /california-parks/article/muir-woods-national-park-history-timeline-project-16414800 .php.

15. Michael Brune, "Pulling Down Our Monuments," *Sierra Club*, July 22, 2020, https:// www.sierraclub.org/michael-brune/2020/07/john-muir-early-history-sierra-club.

16. Harrell, "Muir Woods Park Staff Annotates Own Signs."

17. Interview with Debbie Reese conducted March 1, 2023.

18. National Park Service, "How Women Saved Muir Woods," June 3, 2021, https:// www.nps.gov/articles/how-women-saved-muir-woods.htm.

19. National Park Service, "The Kent Family and Conservation," October 28, 2021, https://www.nps.gov/articles/the-kent-family-and-conservation.htm.

20. Henry Louis Gates Jr., "Who's Afraid of Black History," *New York Times*, February 17, 2023, https://www.nytimes.com/2023/02/17/opinion/desantis-florida-african -american-studies-black-history.html; and Jill Lepore, "Why the School Wars Still Rage," *New Yorker*, March 14, 2022, https://www.newyorker.com/magazine/2022/03 /21/why-the-school-wars-still-rage.

21. Interview with Reese.

22. I model my approach after the scholarship of colleague Manuel Espinoza, and his co-authors, who offer empirical "notes on the study of dignity." Profe Espinoza and colleagues suggest that a noun—like the concept of dignity—is, alternatively, an everyday activity; as such, they "call it forth as a social verb." My approach to annotation is similar. See: Manuel Espinoza et al., "Matters of Participation: Notes on the Study of Dignity and Learning," *Mind, Culture, and Activity* 27, no. 4 (2020): 325–326.

23. Recent works in this area are mentioned in Stauffer, *Book Traces*, 7.

24. Jackson, *Marginalia*, 265.

25. In this book, I am not concerned with annotation in the natural sciences (as with annotated genomes), or with annotation in computer science (as with labeling data, machine learning, or AI), though for a brief discussion see chapter 2 ("Annotation Provides Information") in Kalir and Garcia, *Annotation*.

NOTES TO CHAPTER 1 147

26. See for example: Xinran Zhu et al., "Reading and Connecting: Using Social Annotation in Online Classes," *Information and Learning Sciences* 121, no. 5/6 (2020): 261–271.

27. For a general review, see chapter 6 ("Annotation Aids Learning") in Kalir and Garcia, *Annotation.*

28. Regarding K–12 education, see: Lauren Zucker, "Under Discussion: Teaching Speaking and Listening," *English Journal* 105, no. 5 (2016): 92–94; and Jolene Zywica and Kimberley Gomez, "Annotating to Support Learning in the Content Areas: Teaching and Learning Science," *Journal of Adolescent and Adult Literacy* 52, no. 2 (October 2008): 155–165. Regarding higher education, see: Mary Traester, Chris Kervina, and Noel Holton Brathwaite, "Pedagogy to Disrupt the Echo Chamber: Digital Annotation as Critical Community to Promote Active Reading," *Pedagogy* 21, no. 2 (April 1, 2021): 329–349.

29. For instance: Jeremiah Kalir et al., "'When I Saw My Peers Annotating': Student Perceptions of Social Annotation for Learning in Multiple Courses," *Information and Learning Sciences* 121, no. 3/4 (2020): 207–230.

30. Gavin Porter, "Collaborative Online Annotation: Pedagogy, Assessment and Platform Comparisons," *Frontiers in Education* 7 (2022).

31. Marissa E. Kwan Lin, "Using an Online Social Annotation Tool in a Content-Based Instruction (CBI) Classroom," *International Journal of TESOL Studies* 3, no. 2 (2021): 5–22.

32. Allison S. Walker, "Perusall: Harnessing AI Robo-tools and Writing Analytics to Improve Student Learning and Increase Instructor Efficiency," *Journal of Writing Analytics* 3 (2019): 227–263.

33. Politics of Learning Writing Collective, "The Learning Sciences in a New Era of US Nationalism," *Cognition and Instruction* 35, no. 2 (2017): 94.

34. See Kalir and Garcia, *Annotation*, 132–136.

35. Jeremiah Kalir, "Social Annotation, Critical Literacy, and Justice-Directed Educator Learning," in *Proceedings of the 2021 Society for Information Technology & Teacher Education International Conference*, ed. Elizabeth Langran and Leanna Archambault (Waynesville, NC: AACE, 2021), 1073.

36. Shannon Mattern, *Code and Clay, Data and Dirt: Five Thousand Years of Urban Media* (Minneapolis, MN: University of Minnesota Press, 2017), xii.

37. Indigenous Sign Initiative, "About," accessed October 14, 2023, https://web .archive.org/web/20230523001713/https://www.indigenoussigninitiative.com/about.

38. John Stilgoe, *Outside Lies Magic: Regaining History and Awareness in Everyday Places* (New York: Walker and Company, 1998), 6.

39. Kate Pahl and Jennifer Rowsell, *Living Literacies: Literacy for Social Change* (Cambridge, MA: MIT Press, 2020), 13.

40. Cherise McBride, Jeremiah Kalir, and Christina Cantrill, "Justice-Oriented Media Literacy in Professional Learning," in *Language, Literacy, Youth, and Culture: Bloomsbury*

Encyclopedia of Social Justice in Education, ed. Arturo Cortez and José R. Lizárraga (London: Bloomsbury, in press).

41. Kalir and Garcia, *Annotation*, 6, 116–117.

42. Jackson, *Marginalia*, 45.

43. Tim Ingold, *Lines* (New York: Routledge, 2007), 44.

44. Michelle Caswell, Ricardo Punzalan, and T-Kay Sangwand, "Critical Archival Studies: An Introduction," *Journal of Critical Library and Information Studies* 1, no.2 (2017): 3.

45. Amy Stornaiuolo, Anna Smith, and Nathan C. Phillips, "Developing a Transliteracies Framework for a Connected World," *Journal of Literacy Research* 49, no. 1 (2017): 70.

46. Victor Ray, "The Racial Politics of Citation," *Inside Higher Ed*, April 27, 2018, https://www.insidehighered.com/advice/2018/04/27/racial-exclusions-scholarly-citations-opinion.

47. An Anonymous Scholar, "Citational Justice and the Growth of Knowledge," *Areo*, December 19, 2019, https://areomagazine.com/2019/12/19/citational-justice-and-the-growth-of-knowledge/; and Diana Kwon, "The Rise of Citational Justice," *Nature* 603, no. 7902 (2022): 568–571.

48. Sara Ahmed, *Living a Feminist Life* (Durham, NC: Duke University Press, 2017); see note 8 from Ahmed's introduction that states, in part: "This policy relates to the intellectual horizon of the book rather than the cultural materials upon which I draw," 270.

49. Ahmed, *Living a Feminist Life*, 16.

50. Stauffer, *Book Traces*, 7.

51. Jackson, *Marginalia*, 6.

52. For example: Stephen Frosh and Lisa Baraitser, "Marginalia," *Qualitative Research in Psychology* 5, no. 1 (2008): 68–77.

53. Catherine D'Ignazio and Lauren Klein, "Our Values and Our Metrics for Holding Ourselves Accountable," in *Data Feminism* (Cambridge, MA: MIT Press, 2020), https://data-feminism.mitpress.mit.edu/pub/3hxh4l8o/release/2.

54. These percentages are inherently imprecise because my citation audit was based on publicly available information and biographies. I counted every individual named and referenced in this book only once—excluding friends and colleagues thanked in my acknowledgments, editors of scholarly volumes, and fictitious or anonymous individuals—despite the fact that I mention some individuals prominently, some people appear in different contexts across multiple chapters, and that I've referenced multiple publications authored by some scholars. I will gladly share my detailed citation audit upon request, and I hope that other researchers interested in annotation and critical literacy embrace and further refine similar methods within their scholarship.

CHAPTER 2

1. Gerry Hazelton, *Harriet Tubman* (House of Representative Report No. 787, 43d Congress, 1st Session, Washington, DC, 1874).

NOTES TO CHAPTER 2

2. Archives, "The 'Very Deserving Case' of Harriet Tubman," United States House of Representatives, March 30, 2021, https://history.house.gov/Blog/2021/March/3 -30-Tubman/. See also the 1898 letter from US Representative Sereno E. Payne that states, "For all her services she only received about $200 during the entire war." US House of Representatives, "Letter from Sereno E. Payne, Chairman of the Committee on Merchant Marine and Fisheries, to George Ray, Chairman of the Committee on Invalid Pensions, on Behalf of the Claim of Harriet Tubman that She was Employed as a Nurse, Cook, and a Spy," National Archives and Records Administration, February 5, 1898, https://catalog.archives.gov/id/306574.

3. Kate Clifford Larson, *Bound for the Promised Land: Harriet Tubman: Portrait of an American Hero* (New York: One World, 2004), 252; and Clarence Lusane, *Twenty Dollars and Change: Harriet Tubman and the Ongoing Fight for Racial Justice and Democracy* (San Francisco: City Lights Books, 2022), 3.

4. Nell Irvin Painter, *Creating Black Americans: African-American History and Its Meanings, 1619 to the Present* (New York: Oxford University Press, 2007), 130.

5. Erica Armstrong Dunbar, *She Came to Slay: The Life and Times of Harriet Tubman* (New York: Simon & Schuster, 2019), 91–95.

6. Catherine Clinton, *Harriet Tubman: The Road to Freedom* (New York: Little, Brown and Company, 2004), 202; Lusane, *Twenty Dollars and Change*, 3.

7. Kate Clifford Larson, "Harriet Tubman: A Life Beyond Myths," *Ms.*, February 8, 2022, https://msmagazine.com/2022/02/08/harriet-tubman-life-myth-misinformation-civil -rights-slavery/.

8. Larson, "Harriet Tubman: A Life beyond Myths."

9. Veterans Administration, "Approved Pension File for Harriet Tubman Davis, Widow of Private Nelson Davis (alias Nelson Charles), Company G, 8th U.S. Colored Troops Infantry Regiment (WC-415288)," National Archives and Records Administration, ca. 1890–ca. 1934, https://catalog.archives.gov/id/5939992; hereafter referred to as "Tubman Pension File."

10. Larson, *Bound for the Promised Land*, 277.

11. Tubman Pension File, "Declaration for Widow's Pension," 27. This Pension Bureau form, dated July 14, 1890, notes: "The Act of June 27, 1890, requires, in widow's case," and then lists five criteria.

12. Tubman Pension File: 10, "death;" 13, "marriage;" 14, "death 1st husband;" 19, "death 1st husband;" 29, "comrade identity;" 31, "no divorce;" 34, "no prior marriage. Sold;" 38, "H & Lot 12 or 14 hundred dollars;" 40, "no means of support but labor, no re-marriage;" 49, "no prior mar Sold;" 57, "no divorce;" 95, "Assment record;" 105, "no prior services;" and 107, "comrade identity."

13. Jean Humez, *Harriet Tubman: The Life and the Life Stories* (Madison, WI: University of Wisconsin Press, 2003), 109–110.

14. Donald R. Shaffer, *After the Glory: The Struggles of Black Civil War Veterans* (Lawrence, KS: University Press of Kansas, 2000), 133. Shaffer also observes: "Nearly 84 percent of the white widows managed to receive pensions, while only around

61 percent of African American widows made at least one successful application, a 23-percent gap," 134.

15. Larry Logue and Peter Blanck, "'Benefit of the Doubt': African-American Civil War Veterans and Pensions," *Journal of Interdisciplinary History* 38, no. 3 (2008): 379.

16. Clinton, *Harriet Tubman,* 206.

17. US House of Representatives, "General Affidavit of Harriet Tubman Relating to Her Claim for a Pension," National Archives and Records Administration, 1898, https://catalog.archives.gov/id/306573.

18. US House of Representatives, "Petition of the Residents of Auburn, New York, Requesting that the claim of Harriet Tubman be Called Up," National Archives and Records Administration, 1898, https://catalog.archives.gov/id/306577.

19. US House of Representatives, "H.R. 4982, A Bill Granting a Pension to Harriet Tubman Davis, Late a Nurse in the U.S. Army," National Archives and Records Administration, January 19, 1899, https://catalog.archives.gov/id/306578.

20. Tubman Pension File, "House of Representatives Report No. 1774," 23–24.

21. Dunbar, *She Came to Slay,* 27.

22. US Senate, "Report No. 1619: Harriet Tubman Davis," National Archives and Records Administration, February 7, 1899, https://www.archives.gov/files/legislative /resources/education/tubman/images/srpt_1619-xl.jpg.

23. Lusane, *Twenty Dollars and Change,* 321.

24. Treasury Department, "An Open Letter from Secretary Lew," *Medium,* April 20, 2016, https://medium.com/@USTreasury/an-open-letter-from-secretary-lew-672cfd5 91d02.

25. It is coincidental that Tubman's approved widow's pension was $20 a month, and, subsequently, that she was ultimately selected—through a popular voting campaign organized by the Women on 20s nonprofit organization—to appear on the new $20 banknote. For more information about Women on 20s, see: https://www.womenon20s .org/about.

26. Lusane contextualizes the Tubman twenty amidst broader racial justice concerns and considers public symbolism within "today's movements to dismantle white privilege, end police violence, achieve fairness in health care and medicine, and expand and protect memory, free speech, and voting for all;" *Twenty Dollars and Change,* 125.

27. Clarence Lusane, "What We'll Be Celebrating When Harriet Tubman Appears on the 20-Dollar Bill," *Nation,* March 31, 2023, https://www.thenation.com/article /society/harriet-tubman-twenty-dollar-bill/.

28. Lusane, *Twenty Dollars and Change,* 17.

29. Brittney Cooper, "Putting Harriet Tubman on the $20 Bill Is Not a Sign of Progress. It's a Sign of Disrespect," *Time,* January 27, 2021, https://time.com/5933920 /harriet-tubman-20-bill-joe-biden/. See also: Steven Thrasher, "To Put Harriet Tubman on the $20 Bill Would be an Insult to Her Legacy," *The Guardian,* May 15, 2015,

https://www.theguardian.com/commentisfree/2015/may/15/a-slave-abolitionist-has
-no-business-being-on-the-20-bill.

30. Lusane, *Twenty Dollars and Change,* 323.

31. Genevieve B. Tung and Ruth Anne Robbins, "Beyond #TheNew10—The Case for a Citizens Currency Advisory Committee," *Rutgers University Law Review* 69, no. 195 (2016), 197.

32. See "Harriet Tubman Stamp," https://tubmanstamp.com/.

33. DeNeen L. Brown, "Harriet Tubman Is Already Appearing on $20 Bills Whether Trump Officials Like It or Not," *Washington Post,* May 23, 2019, https://www
.washingtonpost.com/history/2019/05/24/harriet-tubman-is-already-appearing-bills
-whether-trump-officials-like-it-or-not/.

34. "Trump Admin Stall on Tubman $20 Bill Inspires DIY Solution | Maddow | MSNBC," YouTube, https://www.youtube.com/watch?v=myoRLqj7vJQ.

35. Lusane, *Twenty Dollars and Change,* 23.

36. US Department of Transportation Federal Highway Administration, "Harriet Tubman Underground Railroad Byway," accessed January 20, 2023, https://fhwaapps
.fhwa.dot.gov/bywaysp/StateMaps/Show/byway/2260.

37. Harriet Tubman Underground Railroad Byway, "Driving Tour Guide," 2017, 5. Available online at http://harriettubmanbyway.org/newhtbw/wp-content/uploads
/2017/03/TubmanBywayGuide_2017.pdf.

38. Anne Kyle, "Interpreting Harriet Tubman's Life on a Silent Landscape," *National Trust for Historic Preservation: Preservation Leadership Forum,* October 13, 2017, https://
web.archive.org/web/20210617213606/https://forum.savingplaces.org/blogs/special
-contributor/2017/10/13/interpreting-harriet-tubmans-life-on-a-silent-landscape#.

39. The White House, "Presidential Proclamation—Harriet Tubman Underground Railroad National Monument," March 25, 2013, https://obamawhitehouse.archives
.gov/the-press-office/2013/03/25/presidential-proclamation-harriet-tubman
-underground-railroad-national-m.

40. Harriet Tubman Underground Railroad Byway, 5

41. Martha S. Jones, "Finding Traces of Harriet Tubman on Maryland's Eastern Shore," *New York Times,* June 21, 2022, https://www.nytimes.com/2022/06/21/travel
/harriet-tubman-maryland.html.

42. Harriet Tubman Underground Railroad Byway, 5.

43. Admittedly, one of my excursions along the Tubman Byway was waylaid when the truck's shift cable detached at the Denton Steamboat Wharf and my fieldwork was rerouted to 404 Auto Repair.

44. Kyle, "Interpreting Harriet Tubman's Life on a Silent Landscape."

45. The website Historical Marker Database includes a collection titled "Harriet Tubman Underground Railroad Byway Historical Markers," with entries that feature crowdsourced photographs of many markers and the markers' inscriptions; accessed January 20, 2023, https://www.hmdb.org/results.asp?Search=Series&SeriesID=272.

46. Kate Clifford Larson, email message to author, January 31, 2023.

47. Harriet Tubman Underground Railroad Byway, "Virtual Reality Experiences Bring Powerful Stories to Life," accessed March 27, 2023, https://harriettubmanbyway.org /virtual-reality-experiences-enhance-byway-sites/.

48. Mark Priest, email message to author, April 20, 2023.

49. April O'Brien, "Exclusionary Public Memory Documents: Orienting Historical Marker Texts within a Technical Communication Framework," *Technical Communication Quarterly* 31, no. 2 (2022), 112.

50. Clint Smith, *How the Word Is Passed: A Reckoning with the History of Slavery Across America* (New York: Little, Brown and Company, 2021), 367–368.

51. Catherine Squires and Aisha Upton, "Redesigning a Pocket Monument: A Reparative Reading of the 2016 Twenty-Dollar-Bill Controversy," in *Racialized Media: The Design, Delivery, and Decoding of Race and Ethnicity,* eds. Matthew Hughey and Emma González-Lesser (New York: New York University Press, 2020), 52, 54.

52. Lusane, *Twenty Dollars and Change,* 41.

53. Tubman Pension File 4, 8, 26, 36, 42, 55, 60, 93.

54. Tiya Miles, "'Come Out and See the Stars:' How Americans like Harriet Tubman Found Hope in Nature, *Atlantic,* September 12, 2023, https://www.theatlantic.com /ideas/archive/2023/09/harriet-tubman-tiya-miles-wild-girls/675285/.

CHAPTER 3

1. Lizbeth De La Cruz Santana, "The Playas de Tijuana Mural Project: Digital Storytelling, Portraiture, and U.S.-Mexico Border Art," in *Critical Storytelling from the Borderlands En la Línea,* eds. Carmella Braniger and Julio Enríquez-Ornelas (Leiden, Netherlands: Brill, 2022), 38. In this chapter, quotes of De La Cruz Santana's scholarship are cited with notes; other quotes of De La Cruz Santana are from my interview with her conducted March 16, 2023.

2. Lizbeth De La Cruz Santana, "The Playas de Tijuana Mural Project," 31.

3. Lizbeth De La Cruz Santana, *Playas de Tijuana Mural Project Information Kit* (2021), 4.

4. To be clear, the United States provoked this war and invaded Mexico in 1846. The war resulted in the theft and subsequent occupation of half of Mexico's territory. And the Treaty of Guadalupe Hidalgo's contested enforcement has resulted in considerable losses of land, as well as political and cultural rights, for both Mexicans and Indigenous peoples. See, for example: Rodolfo Acuña, *Occupied America: A History of Chicanos* (New York: Pearson Longman, 2007), 42–51; and Ramón A. Gutiérrez and Elliott Young, "Transnationalizing Borderlands History," *Western Historical Quarterly* 41, no. 1 (2010): 39–41.

5. Wendy Chase, "Tijuana Dreams: An Interview with Lizbeth De La Cruz Santana," *Interdisciplinary Humanities* 36, no. 3 (2019): 137.

6. National Building Museum, *The Wall/El Muro,* 2023, Washington, DC.

NOTES TO CHAPTER 3

7. Gloria Anzaldúa, *Borderlands/La Frontera: The New Mestiza* (San Francisco: Aunt Lute Books, 1987), 3.

8. Paula Rebert, *La Gran Línea: Mapping the United States-Mexico Boundary, 1849–1857* (Austin: University of Texas Press, 2001), 2.

9. William H. Emory, *Report of the United States and Mexico Boundary Survey, Made Under Direction of the Secretary of the Interior* (Senate Executive Document No. 108, 34th Congress, 1st Session, Washington, DC, 1857), 32.

10. For a comprehensive history of border fencing and wall construction as "compensatory building" by the US government, see chapters 3 and 4 in C. J. Alvarez, *Border Land, Border Water: A History of Construction on the US-Mexico Divide* (Austin: University of Texas Press, 2019).

11. C. J. Alvarez, *Border Land, Border Water*, 9.

12. Katherine G. Morrissey, "Monuments, Photographs, and Maps: Visualizing the U.S.-Mexico Border in the 1890s," in *Border Spaces: Visualizing the U.S.-Mexico Frontera*, eds. Katherine G. Morrissey and John-Michael H. Warner (Tucson: The University of Arizona Press, 2018), 41.

13. Among recent books that address these topics, see: Camilla Fojas, *Border Optics: Surveillance Cultures on the US-Mexico Frontier* (New York: New York University Press, 2021); Jason De León, *The Land of Open Graves: Living and Dying on the Migrant Trail* (Oakland: University of California Press, 2015); Nicole Torres, *Walls of Indifference: Immigration and the Militarization of the US-Mexico Border* (New York: Routledge, 2016); and Eileen Traux, *We Built the Wall: How the US Keeps Out Asylum Seekers from Mexico, Central America, and Beyond* (London: Verso, 2018).

14. Norma Iglesias Prieto, "Transborderisms: Practices That Tear Down Walls," in *Borderwall as Architecture: A Manifesto for the U.S.-Mexico Boundary*, ed. Ronald Rael (Oakland: University of California Press, 2017), 23.

15. Article V mentions a "copy" of two different maps, yet the meaning of "copy" differs significantly. The Plan of the Port of San Diego "copy" was an original tracing of Pantoja's 1782 map printed in an 1802 atlas. That's not the case with "the map entitled 'Map of the United Mexican States, as organized and defined by various acts of the Congress of said republic, and constructed according to the best authorities. Revised edition. Published in New York, in 1847, by J. Disturnell.'" When the treaty was signed, Americans used the seventh edition of Disturnell's 1847 map as their treaty map, whereas Mexicans used the twelfth edition: "It is not likely that the negotiators realized that they had placed two different editions of Disturnell's map with the treaty, but the differences between the two editions apparently caused no complications in the boundary survey" (Rebert, *La Gran Línea*, 6). Despite attaching different Disturnell editions to respective versions of the authenticated treaty, neither were hand-drawn traces (like Pantoja).

16. Rebert, *La Gran Línea*, 17–18; see also Rachel St. John, *Line in the Sand: A History of the Western U.S.-Mexico Border* (Princeton: Princeton University Press, 2011), 23–27.

17. Data on border crossing into the US are summarized by the Bureau of Transportation Statistics: https://data.bts.gov/stories/s/Tables-Query-Tool/6rt4-smhh.

18. John Stilgoe, *What Is Landscape?* (Cambridge, MA: MIT Press, 2015), 1.

19. US Customs and Border Protection determined that barriers at Playas de Tijuana were no longer structurally sound. CBP announced in January of 2023 that it would replace the deteriorated barriers with a thirty-foot wall. See "Border Barrier From Yogurt Canyon to Imperial Beach (Friendship Circle)—San Diego County—September 2022," US Customs and Border Protection, published January 17, 2023, https://www.cbp.gov/document/environmental-assessments/border-barrier-yogurt-canyon-imperial-beach-friendship-circle.

20. Alexandra Mendoza, "Old San Diego-Tijuana Border Fence at Beach Demolished to Make Way for New Barrier," *San Diego Union-Tribune*, August 7, 2023, https://www.sandiegouniontribune.com/news/border-baja-california/story/2023-08-07/old-san-diego-tijuana-border-fence-at-beach-begins-to-come-down-to-make-way-for-new-barrier.

21. One anonymous reviewer of this book's manuscript suggested that I consider what the US border wall has "in common with the wall separating East and West Berlin." To guide readers' attention to examples of re/marks from another cultural and historical context, consider viewing the Berlin Wall Foundation's online photography collection that includes dozens of examples of "Mauerreste" (remains of wall) and "Mauerelemente" (wall elements) marked with murals, graffiti, paint, tags, peace signs, and phrases like "East-West Unity" and "No More Walls;" see https://sammlung.stiftung-berliner-mauer.de/.

22. Translation: "Let this be a lesson to build a society that tears down walls and builds bridges of solidarity and understanding, always seeking the common good, social justice, freedom, and brotherhood." Alexandra Mendoza, "Portion of Berlin Wall—Once Gifted to the U.S. But Rejected by Trump—Now Stands in Tijuana," *San Diego Union-Tribune*, August 15, 2023, https://www.sandiegouniontribune.com/news/border-baja-california/story/2023-08-15/berlin-wall-tijuana.

23. US Congress, *The Treaty Between the United States and Mexico* (30th Congress, 1st Session, Executive No. 52, Washington, DC, 1848), 91.

24. In contrast to boundary maps created after a ground survey, we are concerned with a "treaty map." According to Rebert, "Maps consulted during negotiations and mentioned in the treaty are known as treaty maps." See: Paula Rebert, "Drawing the Line," in *Mapping Latin America: A Cartographic Reader*, eds. Jordana Dym and Karl Offen (Chicago: University of Chicago Press, 2011), 160.

25. Rebert, *La Gran Línea*, 9.

26. A comprehensive account of negotiations, including debate about San Diego with references to diplomatic correspondences and primary documents, is summarized in Hunter Miller, *Treaties and Other International Acts of the United States of America*, Vol. 5 (Washington, DC: Department of State, 1937), 315–338.

27. Miller, *Treaties and Other International Acts*, 337.

NOTES TO CHAPTER 3

28. Lawrence Martin, "The Plan of the Port of San Diego," in *Treaties and Other International Acts of the United States of America*, Vol. 5, ed. Hunter Miller (Washington, DC: Department of State, 1937), 371.

29. "A later chart of 1786" is mentioned in the description of Pantoja's map by Barry Lawrence Ruderman Antique Maps, https://www.raremaps.com/gallery/detail/48446 /plano-del-puerto-de-san-diego-situado-en-la-costa-septentrio-pantoja-y-arriaga; see also Martin's comment that "Still another copy seems to have been the basis . . ." in "The Plan of the Port of San Diego," 371.

30. Martin, "The Plan of the Port of San Diego," 371.

31. Josef Espinosa y Tello, *Atlas Para el Viage de Las Goletas Sutil y Mexicana al Reconocimiento del Estrecho de Juan de Fuca en 1792* (Madrid: Imprenta Real, 1802). An open access version of this atlas is available from the University of British Columbia, https://open.library.ubc.ca/collections/bcbooks/items/1.0222772.

32. Josef Espinosa y Tello, *Relación del Viage Hecho por las Goletas Sutil y Mexicana en el Año de 1792 Para Reconocer el Estrecho de Fuca* (Madrid: Imprenta Real, 1802). An open access version of this volume is available from the University of British Columbia, https://open.library.ubc.ca/collections/bcbooks/items/1.0222835.

33. Rebert, *La Gran Línea*, 11.

34. There are differences of punctuation, spelling, and phrasing, as well as the plenipotentiaries' signatures and seals, among the multiple "original" handwritten versions of the treaty, including versions written in both English and Spanish; see Miller, *Treaties and Other International Acts*, 237–240.

35. Frank Williams, "Lawrence Martin 1880–1955," *Annals of the Association of American Geographers* 46, no. 3 (1956): 357–364.

36. Martin, "The Plan of the Port of San Diego," 371.

37. Allen Guelzo, "'War Is a Great Evil': Robert E. Lee in the War with Mexico," *Southwestern Historical Quarterly* 122, no. 1 (2018): 77.

38. Miller, *Treaties and Other International Acts*, 335.

39. I read Lee's handwritten note in the Trist Papers at the Library of Congress (microfilm reel 9, date January 15); see also Martin, "The Plan of the Port of San Diego," 371.

40. Martin, "The Plan of the Port of San Diego," 371.

41. St. John, *Line in the Sand*, 14; see also 21.

42. Various surveying methods described as "running the line" are summarized in Rebert, *La Gran Línea*, 30–32.

43. Translation: "A line is easily drawn on paper with a ruler and pencil; but on land it is not the same." José Salazar Ylarregui, *Datos de los Trabajos Astronomicos y Topograficos, Dispuestos en Forma de Dario* (Mexico City: Imprenta de Juan R. Navarro, 1850), 36.

44. Rebert, *La Gran Línea*, 11; St. John, *Line in the Sand*, 35–37.

45. US Congress, *Report of the Boundary Commission Upon the Survey and Re-Marking of the Boundary Between the United States and Mexico West of the Rio Grande, 1891 to*

1896: Parts 1 and 2 (55th Congress, 2nd Session, Document No. 247, Washington, DC, 1898), 173.

46. Rebert, *La Gran Línea*, 191.

47. An additional eighteen monuments were added in the early 1900s to complement the two-hundred and fifty-eight described here.

48. Alvarez, *Border Land, Border Water*, 21.

49. US Congress, *Report of the Boundary Commission*, 12.

50. Rebert, *La Gran Línea*, 190.

51. US Congress, *Report of the Boundary Commission*, 47–49, 197.

52. Morrissey, "Monuments, Photographs, and Maps," 56.

53. Alvarez, *Border Land, Border Water*, 4.

54. Alvarez, *Border Land, Border Water*, 4.

55. US Congress, *Report of the Boundary Commission*, 197.

56. US Congress, *Report of the Boundary Commission*, 198; Rebert, *La Gran Línea*, 20.

57. Iglesias Prieto, "Transborderisms," 23.

58. De La Cruz Santana, "The Playas de Tijuana Mural Project," 31.

59. The Illegal Immigration Reform and Immigrant Responsibility Act of 1996 established three- and ten-year bars for noncitizen migrants present in the US. The bars prevent migrants from returning to the US after deportation, with the ten-year bar applying to people who had been in the US without legal status for one year or longer; "Three- and Ten-Year Bars: 5 Things You Should Know," *FWD.us*, September 14, 2022, https://www.fwd.us/news/5-things-to-know-about-three-and-ten-year-bars/.

60. A secondary barrier, on the American side of the border, further restricts access to Friendship Park.

61. Rael, *Borderwall as Architecture*, 16.

62. Rael, *Borderwall as Architecture*, 134.

63. Laura Staugaitis, "A Collaboratively Painted 'Mural of Brotherhood' Stretches for over a Mile on Mexico's Border," *Colossal*, June 26, 2019, https://www.thisiscolossal .com/2019/06/mural-of-brotherhood/.

64. Hakim Bishara, "3,800 Volunteers Have Joined an Artist to Challenge Trump's Idea of a 'Big, Beautiful Wall' on the US-Mexico Border," *Hyperallergic*, June 24, 2019, https://hyperallergic.com/506480/3800-volunteers-have-joined-an-artist-to-challenge -trumps-idea-of-a-big-beautiful-wall-on-the-us-mexico-border/.

65. Translation: "We know that all art can be a protest, but we want to do it peacefully as we have always done and leave a positive message to the migrant community, in Tijuana and on the other side of the border." Alexandra Mendoza, "Artistas Pintan el Recién Remplazado Muro Fronterizo en Tijuana," *San Diego Union-Tribune*, October 30, 2023, https://www.sandiegouniontribune.com/en-espanol/noticias/ut-espanol /articulo/2023-10-30/artistas-pintan-el-recien-remplazado-muro-fronterizo-en-tijuana.

NOTES TO CHAPTER 4 157

66. Maria Santana, "Deported Vets Helped Paint this Upside-Down US Flag on the Border. Will They Have to Remove it?" *CNN*, April 20, 2018, https://www.cnn.com /2018/04/20/us/paintings-us-mexico-border-fence/index.html.

67. Miriam Jordan, "Deported Veterans Long to Return from Exile. Some Will Get the Chance," *New York Times*, July 26, 2021, https://www.nytimes.com/2021/07/26 /us/deported-immigrants-us-veterans.html.

68. Alexandra Mendoza, "Murals from the Old Border Wall Were Going to Be Destroyed. Now They Will Be Given New Life," *San Diego Union-Tribune*, March 21, 2024, https://www.sandiegouniontribune.com/news/border-baja-california/story/2024 -03-21/mexico-border-wall-friendship-park-murals-saved-museum.

69. "U.S. Veterans Return to Arizona After Being Deported," *ABC 15 Arizona*, August 24, 2022, https://www.abc15.com/news/state/u-s-veterans-return-to-arizona -after-being-deported.

70. Emily Wax-Thibodeaux, "For Years a Flag Mural at the Border Has Honored Deported U.S. Military Veterans. After Trump's Visit, Agents Are Looking into Taking It Down," *Washington Post*, May 6, 2018, https://www.washingtonpost.com/news/post -nation/wp/2018/05/16/for-years-a-flag-mural-at-the-border-has-honored-deported-u-s -military-veterans-after-trump-visit-agents-are-looking-into-taking-it-down/.

71. Humanizing Deportation, "About the Project," accessed March 21, 2023, http:// humanizandoladeportacion.ucdavis.edu/en/about-the-project/.

72. Chase, "Tijuana Dreams," 142.

73. De La Cruz Santana, "The Playas de Tijuana Mural Project," 39.

74. Rael, *Borderwall as Architecture*, 122.

75. De La Cruz Santana, "The Playas de Tijuana Mural Project," 40.

76. Lizbeth De La Cruz Santana, email message to author, October 3, 2023.

CHAPTER 4

1. "Meet Maya Little, UNC Student Whose Protest Ignited the Movement to Topple a Racist Confederate Statue," *Democracy Now*, August 22, 2018, https://www .democracynow.org/2018/8/22/meet_maya_little_unc_student_whos.

2. Maya Little, "Contextualizing UNC-Chapel Hill's Confederate Monument in Blood," *Facing South*, May 2, 2018, https://www.facingsouth.org/2018/05/voices-contextualizing -unc-chapel-hills-confederate-monument-blood.

3. Adam Domby, *The False Cause: Fraud, Fabrication, and White Supremacy in Confederate Memory* (Charlottesville, VA: University of Virginia Press, 2020), 13.

4. Erin Thompson, *Smashing Statues: The Rise and Fall of America's Public Monuments* (New York: W.W. Norton & Company, 2022), 11.

5. Little, "Contextualizing UNC-Chapel Hill's Confederate Monument in Blood."

6. Jennifer Fernandez, "The Unfinished Story of Silent Sam, From 'Soldier Boy' to Fall Symbol of a Painful Past," *Winston-Salem Journal*, August 25, 2018, https://journalnow

.com/the-unfinished-story-of-silent-sam-from-soldier-boy-to-fallen-symbol-of-a-painful/article_a6acd108-b027-5d1f-8354-32b28d7b34b3.html.

7. University Archives at UNC Chapel Hill, "Graffiti on Silent Sam: 1968 and 2015," *For the Record*, July 9, 2015, https://blogs.lib.unc.edu/uarms/2015/07/09/graffiti-on-silent-sam-1968-and-2015/; University Archives at UNC Chapel Hill, "Timeline," *A Guide to Resources about UNC's Confederate Monument*, https://exhibits.lib.unc.edu/exhibits/show/silent-sam/timeline.

8. Drew Goins, "Silent Sam Spray-Painted Again with Message of Racial Protest," *The Daily Tar Heel*, August 18, 2015, https://www.dailytarheel.com/article/2015/08/silent-sam-spray-painted-again.

9. Charlotte Fryar, "McCorkle Place," *Reclaiming the University of the People*, March, 2019, https://uncofthepeople.com/essays/mccorkle-place/.

10. Goins, "Silent Sam Spray-Painted Again."

11. Roger Hartley, *Monumental Harm: Reckoning with Jim Crow Era Confederate Monuments* (Columbia, SC: The University of South Carolina Press, 2021), 53.

12. Hartley, *Monumental Harm*, 94–95; Domby, *The False Cause*, 13–21.

13. Julian Carr, "Unveiling of Confederate Monument at University," *UNC Libraries*, accessed April 25, 2023, https://exhibits.lib.unc.edu/items/show/5519.

14. *Silence Sam Film*, produced by Ligaiya Romero (2020; Chapel Hill, NC: Students of MEJO 582), https://youtu.be/o9uQKmRipQM.

15. Kirk Savage, *Standing Soldiers, Kneeling Slaves: Race, War, and Monument in Nineteenth-Century America* (Princeton: Princeton University Press, 2018), 210.

16. Allie Kelly and Madi Kirkman, "'It's Important They Understand:' Leaders in Silent Sam Reversal Aim to Educate Next Generation," *The Daily Tar Heel*, September 21, 2022, https://www.dailytarheel.com/article/2022/09/university-silent-sam-reunion.

17. Caroline Randall Williams, "You Want a Confederate Monument? My Body Is a Confederate Monument," *New York Times*, June 26, 2020, https://www.nytimes.com/2020/06/26/opinion/confederate-monuments-racism.html.

18. Catherine Clinton, W. Fitzhugh Brundage, Karen Cox, Gary Gallagher, and Nell Irvin Painter, *Confederate Statues and Memorialization* (Athens, GA: The University of Georgia Press, 2019), 7.

19. Clinton et al., *Confederate Statues and Memorialization*, 66.

20. Derek Alderman, Jordan Brasher, and Owen Dwyer, "Memorials and Monuments," in *International Encyclopedia of Human Geography*, 2nd edition, ed. Audrey Kobayashi (Oxford: Elsevier, 2020), 40.

21. America's memorial landscape continues to change years after these demonstrations, as with the 2023 melting of the Robert E. Lee statue that once stood in Charlottesville; see Erin Thompson, "The Most Controversial Statue in America Surrenders to the Furnace," *New York Times*, October 27, 2023, https://www.nytimes.com/2023/10/27/opinion/robert-e-lee-confederate-statues.html.

NOTES TO CHAPTER 4

22. Monument Lab, *National Monument Audit* (Philadelphia: Monument Lab, 2021), 1; see also https://monumentlab.com/audit.

23. Monument Lab, *National Monument Audit*, 25.

24. Monument Lab, *National Monument Audit*, 11.

25. Other features of the US memorial landscape, including place-names, symbols like flags, as well as heritage sites associated with military bases and cemeteries are beyond the scope of this chapter.

26. Hartley, *Monumental Harm*, 147–149.

27. Alderman, Brasher, and Dwyer, "Memorials and Monuments," 40.

28. Thompson in *Smashing Statues* writes, "Taking down a monument doesn't erase history—but it does remove honor. It shows that the version of history put forward by the monument is no longer the one to which the community wants to signal its allegiance," 171. See also Hartley, *Monumental Harm,* chapter 4; and Domby, *The False Cause,* chapters 1 and 5.

29. As with prior chapters, I read literature about monuments from multiple disciplines to better understand annotation as a literacy practice. As a complement to quoted and referenced texts, I also consulted various secondary sources including: Ana Lucia Araujo, *Slavery in the Age of Memory: Engaging the Past* (New York: Bloomsbury Academic, 2021); Erika Doss, *Memorial Mania: Public Feeling in America* (Chicago: University of Chicago Press, 2010); Paul Farber and Ken Lum, *Monument Lab: Creative Speculations for Philadelphia* (Philadelphia: Temple University Press, 2020); and Alex von Tunzelmann, *Fallen Idols* (London: Headline Publishing Group, 2021).

30. Sarah Maslin Nir and Jeffery May, "Christopher Columbus Statue in Central Park is Vandalized," *New York Times*, September 12, 2017, https://www.nytimes.com/2017 /09/12/nyregion/christopher-columbus-statue-central-park-vandalized.html.

31. Donald J. Trump, "Executive Order on Protecting American Monuments, Memorials, and Statues and Combating Recent Criminal Violence," June 26, 2020, accessed May 17, 2023, https://trumpwhitehouse.archives.gov/presidential-actions/executive -order-protecting-american-monuments-memorials-statues-combating-recent -criminal-violence/.

32. Thompson, *Smashing Statues*, 107.

33. Karen Cox, *No Common Ground: Confederate Monuments and the Ongoing Fight for Racial Justice* (Chapel Hill: The University of North Carolina Press, 2021), 160.

34. Brooklyn Dance, "'They Were Racists': Confederate Monument Found Vandalized in Centennial Park," *The Tennessean,* June 20, 2019, https://www.tennessean.com /story/news/2019/06/17/nashville-confederate-monument-vandalized-centennial -park/1475708001/.

35. Mora J. Beauchamp-Byrd, "Joiri Minaya's *Cloaking of the Statue of Christopher Columbus* (2019): Redressing and Cleaning," *Revista: Harvard Review of Latin America*, August 24, 2021, https://revista.drclas.harvard.edu/joiri-minayas-cloaking-of-the -statue-of-christopher-columbus/.

36. Associated Press, "Raleigh Man Charged with Littering after Putting White Hoods on Capitol Confederate Statue," *North Carolina Public Radio*, March 5, 2019, https://www.wunc.org/race-demographics/2019-03-05/raleigh-man-charged-with-littering-after-putting-white-hoods-on-capitol-confederate-statue.

37. Southern Poverty Law Center, *Whose Heritage? Map*, 2023, accessed January 5, 2024, https://www.splcenter.org/whose-heritage-map.

38. For information about The Kudzu Project see https://www.thekudzuproject.org/; regarding yarn bombing, see Mandy Moore and Leanne Prain, *Yarn Bombing: The Art of Crochet and Knit Graffiti* (Vancouver: Arsenal Press, 2009).

39. Heather Shirey and David Todd Lawrence, "Documenting a Global Uprising through Protest Art in the Street," *Monument Lab* (blog), September 29, 2021, https://monumentlab.com/bulletin/documenting-a-global-uprising-through-protest-art-in-the-streets.

40. Lee's opposition to such monuments is well-documented. Regarding this monument's commissioning, extravagant days-long dedication in May, 1890, resistance among local Black communities, and more contemporary controversies see: Cox, *No Common Ground*, 43–45; Hartley, *Monumental Harm*, 41–46; Savage, *Standing Soldiers, Kneeling Slaves*, 133–155; and American Civil War Museum, *On Monument Avenue*, accessed May 17, 2023, https://onmonumentave.com/onlineexhibits.

41. Thessaly La Force, Zoë Lescaze, Nancy Hass, and M. H. Miller, "The 25 Most Influential Works of American Protest Art Since World War II," *New York Times Style Magazine*, October 15, 2020, https://www.nytimes.com/2020/10/15/t-magazine/most-influential-protest-art.html.

42. Tubman's quote begins: "I grew up like a neglected weed, ignorant of liberty, having no experience of it. Then I was not happy or contented." See Benjamin Drew, *A North-side View of Slavery: The Refugee: Or, The Narratives of Fugitive Slaves in Canada. Related by Themselves, with an Account of the History and Condition of the Colored Population of Upper Canada* (Boston: John P. Jewett and Company, 1856), 30.

43. Jessica Stewart, "Powerful BLM Video Projections Help Reclaim Controversial Robert E. Lee Monument [Interview]," *My Modern Met*, July 28, 2020, https://mymodernmet.com/light-projections-robert-e-lee-memorial/.

44. Reclaiming the Monument, "About Us," accessed May 17, 2023, https://www.reclaimingthemonument.com/copy-of-about-us.

45. Cox, *No Common Ground*, 170.

46. Chelsey R. Carter, "Racist Monuments Are Killing Us," *Museum Anthropology* 41, no. 2: 141.

47. Thompson, *Smashing Statues*, xx.

48. Hartley, *Monumental Harm*, 135.

49. Carter, "Racist Monuments Are Killing Us," 141.

50. Thompson, *Smashing Statues*, 138.

NOTES TO CHAPTER 4 161

51. Caroline Janney, "Written in Stone: Gender, Race, and the Heyward Shepherd Memorial," *Civil War History* 52, no. 2: 139.

52. Real Silent Sam Coalition, "Real Silent Sam Proposal, Delivered to Chancellor Thorp Feb 15, 2012," accessed May 9, 2023, https://realsilentsam-blog.tumblr.com/.

53. Anita Wadhwani, "Nashville Confederate Monument to Stay," *Tennessee Lookout*, February 20, 2023, https://tennesseelookout.com/2023/02/20/nashville-confederate -monument-to-stay/.

54. For an account of these protest actions see: Sinclaire Devereux Marber, "Bloody Foundation? Ethical and Legal Implications of (Not) Removing the Equestrian Statue of Theodore Roosevelt at the American Museum of Natural History," *The Columbia Journal of Law & the Arts* 43, no. 1 (2019): 85–106. Regarding the Anti-Columbus Day Tours, see: Decolonize This Place, *Anti-Columbus Day Tours of the American Museum of Natural History 2016–2019 Reader* (New York, n.d.), https://decolonizethisplace.org/s /Anti-AMNH_Actions-2016-2021_PrinterSpreads_4Website.pdf.

55. Mayoral Advisory Commission on City Art, Monuments, and Markers, "Report to the City of New York," New York, 2018, 25–26.

56. Holland Cotter, "Half-Measures Won't Erase the Painful Past of Our Monuments," *New York Times*, January 12, 2018, https://www.nytimes.com/2018/01/12/arts/design /statues-monuments-deblasio-commission.html.

57. American Museum of Natural History, "Addressing the Statue," accessed May 17, 2023, https://www.amnh.org/exhibitions/addressing-the-statue.

58. Marber, "Bloody Foundation?," 102.

59. Hakim Bishara, "Controversial Roosevelt Monument Doused in Red Paint at American Museum of Natural History," *Hyperallergic*, October 6, 2021, https://hyperallergic .com/682520/roosevelt-monument-doused-in-red-paint-at-american-museum-of -natural-history/.

60. Sarah Bahr, "Roosevelt Statue to Head to Presidential Library in North Dakota," *New York Times*, November 19, 2021, https://www.nytimes.com/2021/11/19/arts /design/roosevelt-statue-north-dakota.html.

61. Theodore Roosevelt Presidential Library Foundation, "Theodore Roosevelt Presidential Library and Roosevelt Descendants Facilitate Loan of Equestrian Statue from City of New York," November 19, 2021, https://www.trlibrary.com/wp-content /uploads/2021/11/TRPL-Announcement-Press-Release-FINAL-1.pdf.

62. Clint Smith, *How the Word Is Passed: A Reckoning with the History of Slavery Across America* (New York: Little, Brown and Company, 2021), 4. Regarding the 2018 addition of markers in New Orleans, see: Rachel Kaufman, "As New Orleans Turns 300, City to Mark Slave Trade Sites," *Next City*, May 10, 2018, https://nextcity.org/urbanist -news/as-new-orleans-turns-300-city-to-mark-slave-trade-sites.

63. James Gill and Howard Hunter, *Tearing Down the Lost Cause: The Removal of New Orleans's Confederate Statues* (Jackson, MS: University Press of Mississippi, 2021). See also: Cox, *No Common Ground*, 158–159; and Hartley, *Monumental Harm*, 4, 6.

64. Unless otherwise stated, all quotes from Amy Dickerson in this section are from my interview with her conducted March 15, 2023.

65. Third Graders of Homer A. Plessy Community School, *Courageous, Eccentric, Diverse: New Monuments for New Orleans* (New Orleans: 826 New Orleans, 2017), 54.

66. Freeman H. M. Murray, *Emancipation and the Freed in American Sculpture* (Washington, DC: Published by the Author, 1916), xix.

67. Detra Price-Dennis and Noelle Mapes, "'I Don't Even Know Why This Is a Monument': Exploring Multimodal Making in Early Childhood," *The Reading Teacher* 75, no. 1: 91–101.

68. Third Graders of Homer A. Plessy Community School, *Courageous, Eccentric, Diverse*, 15.

69. Third Graders, *Courageous, Eccentric, Diverse*, 54.

70. Monument Lab, *National Monument Audit*, 29.

CHAPTER 5

1. Unless referenced otherwise, all quotes of Alex Gino in this chapter are from an interview that Antero Garcia and I conducted with them on October 4, 2021.

2. Alex Gino (@lxgino), "Just a reminder that you officially have my permission to correct your copy of Melissa's Story. Yes, the cover is beautiful. Part of trans justice is to ...," *Twitter*, July 1, 2021, https://twitter.com/lxgino/status/1410607483907821568.

3. Alex Gino, "Melissa's Story and Sharpie Activism," *Alex Gino* (blog), July 10, 2021, http://www.alexgino.com/2021/07/melissas-story-and-sharpie-activism/.

4. American Library Association, "Top 10 Most Challenged Books Lists," *Banned & Challenged Books*, accessed May 22, 2023, https://www.ala.org/advocacy/bbooks/frequentlychallengedbooks/top10.

5. Remi Kalir and Antero Garcia, "#SharpieActivism: Annotating Books as a Movement for Change," *We Need Diverse Books* (blog), December 1, 2021, https://diversebooks.org/sharpieactivism-annotating-books-as-a-movement-for-change/.

6. Joy Kirr (@JoyKirr), "I was finally able to do this on my first day back in the classroom, @lxgino! ...," *Twitter*, August 17, 2021, https://twitter.com/JoyKirr/status/1427759686045081603.

7. Jane Hill (@codenamejane), "I tried to use my best handwriting for our class set, @lxgino! #SharpieActivism," *Twitter*, July 12, 2021, https://twitter.com/codenamejane/status/1414569235934818306.

8. Per Gino's request, I use the book's updated title *Melissa* throughout this chapter, notwithstanding quotes or references to "Melissa's Story" from #SharpieActivism social media posts and related actions.

9. Alex Gino, "Alex Gino Shares the Importance of Changing the Title of *George* to *Melissa*," *On Our Minds* (blog), October 28, 2021, https://oomscholasticblog.com/post/alex-gino-melissa.

NOTES TO CHAPTER 5

10. Jonathan Friedman and Nadine Farid Johnson, "Banned in the USA: Rising School Book Bans Threaten Free Expression and Students' First Amendment Rights," *PEN America*, April, 2022, https://pen.org/banned-in-the-usa/.

11. Kasey Meehan, Tasslyn Magnusson, Sabrina Baêta, and Jonathan Friedman, "Banned in the USA: The Mounting Pressure to Censor," *PEN America*, September 21, 2023, https://pen.org/report/book-bans-pressure-to-censor/.

12. Meehan, "Banned in the USA," with a 33-percent increase in instances of books banned between the two school years; see also an analysis by the *Washington Post* of similar data that found: "A small number of people were responsible for most of the book challenges . . . Individuals who filed 10 or more complaints were responsible for two-thirds of all challenges. In some cases, these serial filers relied on a network of volunteers gathered together under the aegis of conservative parents' groups such as Moms for Liberty;" see Hannah Natanson, "Objection to Sexual LGBTQ Content Propels Spike in Book Challenges," *Washington Post*, May 23, 2023, https://www .washingtonpost.com/education/2023/05/23/lgbtq-book-ban-challengers/.

13. Jonathan Friedman, "Banned in the USA: The Growing Movement to Censor Books in Schools," *PEN America*, September 19, 2022, https://pen.org/report/banned -usa-growing-movement-to-censor-books-in-schools/.

14. See for example: Francesca Paris, "See the States That Have Passed Laws Directed at Young Trans People," *New York Times*, June 5, 2023, https://www.nytimes.com /2023/06/05/upshot/trans-laws-republicans-states.html; and Beth Hawkins, "Scared of School: Even in States with Protective Laws, LGBTQ Students Are Reporting Attacks From Other Kids—and Teachers," *The 74*, May 24, 2023, https://www.the74million .org/article/scared-of-school-even-in-states-with-protective-laws-lgbtq-students-are -reporting-attacks-from-other-kids-and-teachers/.

15. Emily Drabinski, "Queering the Catalog: Queer Theory and the Politics of Correction," *Library Quarterly: Information, Community, Policy* 83, no. 2 (2013): 94.

16. Drabinski, "Queering the Catalog," 105.

17. Drabinski, "Queering the Catalog," 109.

18. Drabinski, "Queering the Catalog," 101.

19. Drabinski, "Queering the Catalog," 97.

20. In LIS literature, classification is often discussed alongside cataloging and the practice of assigning subject headings to books using a controlled vocabulary. For clarity, I do not discuss subject headings in this chapter (whereas classification relies upon notation to physically mark books). Subject headings are metadata added to a book's record in a library catalog to describe the text, represent subjects, and aid search and topical access. Regarding bias in subject headings, see: Sanford Berman, *Prejudices and Antipathies: A Tract on the LC Subject Heads Concerning People* (Jefferson, NC: McFarland & Company, 1993); Matt Johnson, "A Hidden History of Queer Subject Access," in *Radical Cataloging: Essays at the Front,* ed. K. R. Roberto (Jefferson, NC: McFarland & Company, 2008), 18–27; and Katelyn Angell and K. R. Roberto, "Cataloging," *TSQ: Transgender Studies Quarterly* 1, nos. 1–2 (2014), 53–56.

21. Geoffrey C. Bowker and Susan Leigh Star, *Sorting Things Out: Classification and Its Consequences* (Cambridge, MA: MIT Press, 2000), 5.

22. Hope A. Olson, *The Power to Name: Locating the Limits of Subject Representation in Libraries* (Boston: Kluwer Academic Publishers, 2002), 15.

23. Melissa Adler, *Cruising the Library: Perversities in the Organization of Knowledge* (New York: Fordham University Press, 2017), 92.

24. For additional information about the development of these classification schemes, see: Paul Edlund, "A Monster and a Miracle: The Cataloging Distribution Service of the Library of Congress, 1901–1976," *The Quarterly Journal of the Library of Congress* 33, no. 4 (1976): 383–421; and Hope Olson, "The Power to Name: Representation in Library Catalogs," *Signs: Journal of Women in Culture and Society* 26, no. 3 (2001): 639–668.

25. Olson describes library classification as "the notational representation of topics used for the physical and electronic organization of library collections for browsing;" see "The Power to Name," 640.

26. Drabinski, "Queering the Catalog," 98. Regarding alternative classification schemes used by libraries with dedicated queer collections, see: Julia Bullard, Amber Dierking, and Avi Grundner, "Centering LGBT2QIA+ Subjects in Knowledge Organization Systems," *Knowledge Organization* 47, no. 5 (2020): 393–403. Furthermore, as this chapter concerns the classification of books about gender and sexuality, I would be remiss not to mention that LIS scholars have also documented racial bias in classification, see for example: Melissa Adler, "Classification Along the Color Line: Excavating Racism in the Stacks," *Journal of Critical Library and Information Studies* 1, no. 1 (2017), https://journals.litwinbooks.com/index.php/jclis/article/view/17; and Molly Higgins, "Totally Invisible: Asian American Representation in the *Dewey Decimal Classification*, 1876–1996," *Knowledge Organization* 43, no. 8 (2016): 609–621.

27. Melvil Dewey, *Decimal Classification and Relativ Index*, 13th ed. (Essex County, NY: Forest, 1932), 159.9734846.

28. Melvil Dewey, *Dewey Classification and Relative Index*, 17th ed. (New York: Forest, 1965), 268.

29. Sanford Berman, "DDC 19: An Indictment," *Library Journal* 105, no. 5 (1980): 586.

30. Violet Fox, "Updates for LGBT Community and Transgender People," *025.431: The Dewey Blog* (blog), November 16, 2018, https://ddc.typepad.com/025431/2018/11/updates-for-lgbt-community-and-transgender-people.html.

31. Emily Drabinski, "What Is Critical about Critical Librarianship?" *Art Libraries Journal* 44, no. 2 (2019): 51.

32. Melissa Adler, "'Let's Not Homosexualize the Library Stacks': Liberating Gays in the Library Catalog," *Journal of the History of Sexuality* 24, no. 3 (2015): 489.

33. Adler, "'Let's Not Homosexualize the Library Stacks,'" 490.

34. Claire McDonald, "Call Us by Our Name(s): Shifting Representations of the Transgender Community in Classificatory Practice," in *Knowledge Organization at the*

Interface: Proceedings of the Sixteenth International ISKO Conference, eds. Marianne Lykke, Tanja Svarre, Mette Skov, and Danielle Martínez-Ávila (Baden-Baden, DE: Ergon-Verlag, 2020): 290.

35. K. R. Roberto, "Inflexible Bodies: Metadata for Transgender Identities," *Journal of Information Ethics* 20, no. 2 (2011): 56. Regarding one promising development in how libraries can catalogue books by trans authors, see: Amber Billey and Emily Drabinski, "Questioning Authority: Changing Library Cataloging Standards to Be More Inclusive to a Gender Identity Spectrum," *TSQ: Transgender Studies Quarterly* 6, no. 1 (2019): 117–123.

36. Adler, "'Let's Not Homosexualize the Library Stacks,'" 507.

37. Library of Congress, "Gino, Alex. Melissa," LC Name Authority File, accessed June 7, 2023, https://id.loc.gov/authorities/names/no2022130085.html.

38. Drabinski, "What Is Critical about Critical Librarianship?" 50.

39. Drabinski, "What Is Critical about Critical Librarianship?" 53.

40. David Ketchum, "Introduction: Critical Librarianship," in *Critical Librarianship*, eds. Samantha Schmehl Hines and David Ketchum (Bingley, UK: Emerald, 2020), 2. As a comprehensive review of critical librarianship is beyond the scope of this chapter, see also: Maria T. Accardi, Emily Drabinski, and Alana Kumbier (eds.), *Critical Library Instruction: Theories and Methods* (Sacramento: Library Juice Press, 2010); and Sofia Leung and Jorge López-McKnight (eds.), *Knowledge Justice: Disrupting Library and Information Studies Through Critical Race Theory* (Cambridge, MA: MIT Press, 2021).

41. Drabinski, "What Is Critical about Critical Librarianship?" 53.

42. Garden Home Community Library (@gardenhomelib), "You might notice that we've 'defaced' a book in our collection. For the backstory, read author Alex Gino's blog post encouraging people to alter their copies . . . ," *Twitter*, July 16, 2021, https://twitter.com/gardenhomelib/status/1416062452899487744.

43. North Canton Library (@NCantonLibrary), "Did we really just write on a library book? Yup. Why? The author asked us to! Read about Melissa's Story and #Sharpie-Activism here . . . ," *Twitter*, July 18, 2021, https://twitter.com/NCantonLibrary/status/1416847011295416323?.

44. Bloomfield Public Library (@bplct), "From #alexginoauthor: 'Just a reminder that you officially have my permission to correct your copy of Melissa's Story . . . ,'" *Instagram*, September 10, 2021, https://www.instagram.com/p/CTp8BOWJyzP/.

45. Buncombe County Public Libraries (@bcplteen), "We're celebrating acclaimed author, @lxgino and their book, #melissasstory with corrected covers designed by youth librarians in @buncombecounty! . . . ," *Instagram*, October 2, 2021, https://www.instagram.com/p/CUiJg1yrXZz/.

46. Drabinski, "What Is Critical about Critical Librarianship?" 54.

47. This cover was designed by librarian Ashlee Brown of Kenton County Public Library, in Kentucky, and shared on Gino's blog. CPL used this cover's design for the

spine labels of *Melissa* (figure 5.2), and school librarian Christopher Hunt also used Brown's cover to annotate one of his school's two copies.

48. Stoughton Public Library WI (@stoughtonpublibwi), "#weseeyou #goodbydead-name #bewhoyouare #stoughtonpubliclibrary #transgirlsaregirls #stoughtonwi #melis-sasstory #alexgino #booktok #librarytiktok," *TikTok*, July 14, 2021, https://www.tiktok.com/@stoughtonpublibwi/video/6984840557289852165.

49. See for example: Rainbow Round Table, *Open to All: Serving the LGBTQIA+ Community in Your Library* (Chicago: American Library Association, 2022); Sai Deng and Christine Davidian, "Embracing Equity, Diversity and Inclusion (EDI) in Library Cataloging," *Technical Services Quarterly* 38, no. 3 (2021): 315–320; and Jaime Naidoo, "Serving Rainbow Families in School Libraries," in *Intellectual Freedom Issues in School Libraries*, ed. April Dawkins (Santa Barbara: ABC-CLIO, 2020): 186–190.

50. Drabinski, "Queering the Catalog," 104–106.

51. Onondaga Free Library (@onondagafreelib), "We love #sharpieactivism Thanks Alex Gino for writing this beautiful book and for giving it its new perfect title!," *Instagram*, July 30, 2021, https://www.instagram.com/p/CR9xJOLtRaf/.

52. Joseph Kosciw, Caitlin Clark, and Leesh Menard, *The 2021 National School Climate Survey: The Experiences of LGBTQ+ Youth in Our Nation's Schools* (New York: GLSEN, 2022): xxi.

53. Kosciw et al., *The 2021 National School Climate Survey*, 52–53.

54. Erica Hellerstein, "America's Culture Warriors Are Going After Librarians," *Coda*, December 21, 2022, https://www.codastory.com/rewriting-history/war-on-librarians-united-states/.

55. Bridgette Exman, "This Summer, I Became the Book-Banning Monster of Iowa," *New York Times*, September 1, 2023, https://www.nytimes.com/2023/09/01/opinion/book-ban-schools-iowa.html.

56. Carolyn Bailey (@PrincetonMS_LC), "Bring your copy or fix one of ours! #SharpieActivism @lxgino," *Twitter*, September 17, 2021, https://twitter.com/PrincetonMS_LC/status/1438918078662856706.

57. Christopher Hunt, email message to author, May 23, 2023.

58. Remi Kalir, "This School Librarian Fought LGBTQ+ Book Censorship," *We Need Diverse Books* (blog), May 11, 2022, https://diversebooks.org/this-school-librarian-fought-lgbtq-book-censorship/.

CHAPTER 6

1. According to data from the 2021 *National Monument Audit*, see search results for "Harriet Tubman" at: https://monumentlab.github.io/national-monument-audit/app/map.html?q=Harriet%20Tubman&facets=object_groups~Monument__is_duplicate~0&centerLatLon=41.75683%2C-70.08985&startZoom=17.

2. Harriet Tubman Underground Railroad Byway, "New 'Beacon of Hope' Harriet Tubman Statue Finds Permanent Home in Her Homeland," accessed January 5, 2023,

https://harriettubmanbyway.org/new-beacon-of-hope-harriet-tubman-statue-finds-permanent-home-in-her-homeland/.

3. Southern Poverty Law Center, *Whose Heritage? Data Set,* 2023, accessed January 5, 2024, https://docs.google.com/spreadsheets/d/1W4H2qa2THM1ni53QYZftGob_k_Bf9HreFAtCERfjCIU/edit?pli=1#gid=1205021846.

4. Roger Hartley, *Monumental Harm: Reckoning with Jim Crow Era Confederate Monuments* (Columbia, SC: The University of South Carolina Press, 2021), 137.

5. Kate Clifford Larson, *Bound for the Promised Land: Harriet Tubman: Portrait of an American Hero* (New York: One World, 2004), 89.

6. Larson, *Bound for the Promised Land,* 90.

7. Allan Luke, "Critical Literacy: Foundational Notes," *Theory Into Practice* 51, no. 1 (2012): 5.

8. See the summary in: Ernest Morrell, *Critical Literacy and Urban Youth: Pedagogies of Access, Dissent, and Liberation* (New York: Routledge, 2008), 29–55.

9. Paulo Freire and Donald Macedo, *Literacy: Reading the Word and the World* (London: Routledge, 1987).

10. Donald Macedo, *Literacies of Power: What American Are Not Allowed to Know* (Boulder: Westview Press, 1994), 27.

11. Jessica Zacher Pandya et al., "Introduction to the Handbook of Critical Literacies: The Current State of Critical Literacy around the World," in *The Handbook of Critical Literacies,* eds. Jessica Zacher Pandya et al. (New York: Routledge, 2022), 3.

12. Teddy Cruz, "Borderwalls as a Public Scape?" in *Borderwall as Architecture: A Manifesto for the U.S.-Mexico Boundary,* ed. Ronald Rael (Oakland: University of California Press, 2017), xiii.

13. Interview with Courtney McClellan conducted April 4, 2023.

14. I first collaborated with McClellan in the summer of 2021 when we co-facilitated a series of professional development workshops about annotation in partnership with the Library of Congress and the National Council of Teachers of English. See: Remi Kalir, "NCTE Summer Sandbox Explores Speculative Annotation," *National Council of Teachers of English* (blog), September 21, 2021, https://ncte.org/blog/2021/09/reflections-ncte-2021-summer-sandbox-speculative-annotation/.

15. Kris D. Gutiérrez, "Syncretic Approaches to Literacy Learning: Leveraging Horizontal Knowledge and Expertise," in *LRA Yearbook* (2014): 49.

16. José Ramón Lizárraga and Kris D. Gutiérrez, "Centering Nepantla Literacies from the Borderlands: Leveraging 'In-betweenness' Toward Learning in the Everyday," *Theory Into Practice* 57, no. 1 (2018): 38–47.

17. Kris D. Gutiérrez, Andrea Bien, and Makenzie Selland, "Syncretic Approaches to Studying Movement and Hybridity in Literacy Practices," in *Handbook of Research on Teaching the English Language Arts,* 3rd ed., eds. Diane Lapp and Douglas Fisher (New York: Routledge, 2011), 416.

18. Robert Petrone et al., "Youth Civic Participation and Activism (Youth Participatory Action Research)," in *The Handbook of Critical Literacies*, eds. Jessica Zacher Pandya et al. (New York: Routledge, 2022), 50.

19. Kevin Clay and Beth Rubin, "'I Look Deep into This Stuff Because it's a Part of Me': Toward a Critically Relevant Civics Education," *Theory & Research in Social Education* 48, no. 2 (2020): 161–181.

20. Carlos Hipolito-Delgado et al., "Transformative Student Voice for Sociopolitical Development: Developing Youth of Color as Political Actors," *Journal of Research on Adolescence* (2022): 1–11.

21. Nicole Mirra and Antero Garcia, "'I Hesitate But I Do Have Hope': Youth Speculative Civic Literacies for Troubled Times," *Harvard Educational Review* 90, no. 2 (2020): 297.

22. Antero Garcia and Nicole Mirra, "Writing Toward Justice: Youth Speculative Civic Literacies in Online Policy Discourse," *Urban Education* 56, no. 4 (2021): 640–669.

23. Garcia and Mirra, "Writing Toward Justice," 652.

24. US Border Patrol, *Border Patrol Strategic Plan 1994 and Beyond* (Washington, DC: Immigration and Naturalization Service, 1994), 7.

25. Jason De León, *The Land of Open Graves: Living and Dying on the Migrant Trail* (Oakland: University of California Press, 2015), 35.

26. De León, *The Land of Open Graves*, 36; see also National Building Museum, *The Wall/El Muro*, 2023, Washington, DC.

27. Humane Borders, "Migrant Death Mapping," accessed June 23, 2023, https://humaneborders.org/migrant-death-mapping/.

28. Museum of Us, *Hostile Terrain 94*, 2021, San Diego.

29. Mary Aviles, "Data Visualization As an Act of Witnessing," *Nightingale*, March 4, 2020, https://nightingaledvs.com/the-undocumented-migration-project-data-visualization-as-an-act-of-witnessing/.

30. Jason De León and Gabriel Canter, "Portfolio: Hostile Terrain 94," *Theater* 51, no. 1 (2021): 34.

31. Hostile Terrain (@hostileterrain94), "Student @uofmichigan reflecting on a tag they wrote. 'Just a child,'" *Instagram*, May 8, 2019, https://www.instagram.com/p/BxNO0JHFOtt/; Hostile Terrain (@hostileterrain94), "Student Reflecting on writing tags for Hostile Terrain 94," *Instagram*, March 28, 2019, https://www.instagram.com/p/BvkHbmFgDTq/; Hostile Terrain (@hostileterrain94), "Estudiantes de @uofmichigan reflexionando sobre etiquetas que escribieron. 'Lo recordaré,'" *Instagram*, July 3, 2019, https://www.instagram.com/p/BzdgrQ6g3Rc/; and Hostile Terrain (@hostileterrain94), "Una estudiante de @uofmichigan reflexionando sobre una etiqueta que escribio. 'Voy a cumplir 20 años este año. Viviré mi vida recordando que soy bendecida. Descansa en Paz,'" *Instagram*, June 19, 2019, https://www.instagram.com/p/By5TOhbFU13/.

32. Hostile Terrain (@hostileterrain94), "Reflections and reactions from volunteers at HT94 Penn State written on the backs of toe tags," *Instagram*, April 6, 2021, https://www

NOTES TO CHAPTER 6

.instagram.com/p/CNV_euWreHn/; and Hostile Terrain (@hostileterrain94), "Reflections and reactions from volunteers at HT94 Penn State written/drawn on the backs of toe tags," *Instagram*, April 7, 2021, https://www.instagram.com/p/CNYlFmWLROz/.

33. ht94cabrillocollege (@ht94cabrillo), "When we ended the #hostileterrain94 workshop with faculty, each read at least one name aloud. We held space for these incredible people . . . ," *Twitter*, January 23, 2020, https://twitter.com/ht94cabrillo /status/1220222601600983040; and ht94cabrillocollege (@ht94cabrillo), "Today some @CabrilloCollege faculty learned more about #hostileterrain94, brainstormed ways to integrate into their classes . . . ," *Twitter*, January 23, 2020, https://twitter.com /ht94cabrillo/status/1220221151978254336.

34. John Stilgoe, *What Is Landscape?* (Cambridge, MA: MIT Press, 2015), 1.

35. Melissa Adler, "'Let's Not Homosexualize the Library Stacks': Liberating Gays in the Library Catalog," *Journal of the History of Sexuality* 24, no. 3 (2015): 489.

36. Titus Kaphar and Reginald Dwayne Betts, *Redaction* (New York: W.W. Norton, 2023).

37. Shannon Mattern, *Reparative Redaction* (Library Stack, 2023), 7.

38. Camilo Montoya-Galvez, "Veteran Returns to the U.S. After 14-Year Exile Under Biden Effort to Rectify 'Unjust' Deportations," *CBS News*, April 21, 2023, https://www .cbsnews.com/news/deported-veteran-returns-to-us-biden-laura-meza/.

39. San Diego History Center, *History Lab*, 2021, San Diego.

40. Debbie Reese and Jean Mendoza, "About AICL," last modified September 30, 2019, https://americanindiansinchildrensliterature.blogspot.com/p/about.html.

41. Interview with Debbie Reese conducted March 1, 2023.

INDEX

Page numbers in italics refer to figures.

#SharpieActivism, 19–20, 95–105, *101*, 107–112, *109*, *110*, *114*, *115*, 127, 142
#somethingscoming, 78
#UnMundoSinMuros, 62

12 Years a Slave, 91
826 New Orleans, 88, *89*, 90, *90*, *93*, 94, 137
1880 Crow Peace Delegation (Star), 2–3

Adler, Melissa, 102, 104, 135
Ahmed, Sara, 16
Alexander, Elizabeth, 76, 135
Alvarez, C. J., 56, 59
Amby, Lizzie, 37
American Indians in Children's Literature, 140
American Library Association (ALA), 3, 96, 99
American Museum of Natural History (AMNH), 85–86, *87*
Andrew W. Mellon Foundation, 76

Annotation. *See also* Re/marks
as art form, 2–3, 4
call numbers as, 102
children and, 128–129, 139–140
(see also *Courageous, Eccentric, Diverse: New Monuments for New Orleans;* #SharpieActivism)
as civic literacy, 20, 49, 78, 88–91, 130
as critical literacy, 4, 12, 20, 44, 49, 112–117, 125–127
as defacement, 3, 4–5, 78
defined, 11
described, 1–2
in education, 9–10
hybrid and syncretic, 12, 20, 124, 127–130
and impermanence, 14, 49, 72, 79–80, 83, 128–129
and interactivity, 68
layers, 59, 64, 86, 111, 123–125, *124*
(*see also* #SharpieActivism)
negotiated meaning, 12–13
new norms surrounding, 3

172 INDEX

Annotation (cont.)
as non-neutral, 10–12, 135–136
place-based marks (*see* Land-marking)
as protest (*see* Annotation as social activism)
as public dialogue, 4
risks of, 112–113, 117
signatures as, 50, *98* (*see also* Tubman, Harriet, pension file)
social and civic, 12
social life of, 8–12
social rhetoric of, 1–2
street annotation, 5
Annotation and its Texts, 17
Annotation as social activism, 4–7, 71–90, 113, 119–120
as literacy, 78–79
Anti-racist activism, 71–80, *81*
Anzaldúa, Gloria, 47, *50*
Arbery, Ahmaud, 76
Archival traces, CHP 2, CHP 3, beg CHP 4, 15
Atristain, Miguel de, 50

Bailey, Carolyn, 113, *114*, 127
Banned Books Week, 108
Banned in the USA, 97
Bayly House (Cambridge, Maryland), 37, *39*
"Beacon of Hope" statue, 36, 120–123, *121*
Berlin Wall, in Tijuana, 49
Berman, Sanford, 103
Betts, Reginald Dwayne, 135–136
Bibliographic classification, 102–106
and LGBTQIA+ content, 102–103, *105*, *106*
Black Lives Matter, 72, 76, 79
Bloomfield Public Library (Connecticut), 108
Book banning, 3, 96–97
Bookplates, 113, *114*
Book Traces (Stauffer), 2

Borderwall as Architecture: A Manifesto for the U.S.-Mexico Boundary (Rael), 62
Boundary Commissions, 48, 55–56, *57*, *58*
Bowker, Geoffrey, 102
Bowley, Araminta, 122
Bowley, James Alfred, 122
Bowley, John, 122
Bowley, Kessiah Jolley, 122
Brainard, Dorsey, *27*
Brodess Farm, 37, *39*
Bucktown Village Store, 36
Buncombe County Public Libraries (North Carolina), 108

Carr, Julian, 72–73, *74*
Carrera, Mauro, 68
Carter, Chelsey R., 83
Catlett, Elizabeth, 37, *39*
Chiu, Enrique, 62, 68, 126
Choptank Landing, *39*
Choptank River, 36
Christopher Columbus statue (Central Park, New York), 78
Christopher Columbus statue (Minnesota State Capitol), 78–79
Church Creek, 37
Citation and citational practice, 16–17
Classification and cataloging, 100–102
Cleveland, Grover, 31
Clinton, Catherine, 26, 75
Coast Miwok people, 6
Code and Clay, Data and Dirt (Mattern), 10
Combahee Ferry raid, 24
Confederate monuments
Centennial Park (Nashville, Tennessee), 79, 85
Faithful Slave Memorial, 84–85
Nelson County Courthouse (Lovingston, Virginia), *80*
and New Orleans, 88

INDEX

Robert E. Lee Monument (Richmond, Virginia), *81*, *82*
Silent Sam, 19, 71–72, *74*, 85, 126
Whose Heritage? data, 120
Contested (con)texts, 135
Contextualization, 19, 83–88
  Equestrian Statue of Theodore Roosevelt, 86, *87*
  Faithful Slave Memorial, 84–85
Cooper, Brittney, 31
Courageous, Eccentric, Diverse: New Monuments for New Orleans, 88–94, *89–90*, *93*, 127
Couto, José Bernardo, 50
Cox, Karen, 79, 83, 136
Criqui, Alex, 81
Critical context, 139
Critical librarianship, 19–20, 107, 111
Critical literacy, 12, 89, 123–127
  and Confederate monuments, 79, 127
  and #SharpieActivism, 127
  and Tubman, 125, 126
  and the US–Mexico border, 125–126
Cruz, Teddy, 126
Cuauhtli, Chris, 45
Cuevas, Luis Gonzaga, 50
Currency portraits, 1927 memo, *32*

Data Feminism (D'Ignazio and Klein), 17
Davis, Angela, 81
Davis, Nelson, 25, 125
DDC. *See* Dewey Decimal Classification (DDC) system
Deal, Gregg, 11
Decolonize This Place, 85
De La Cruz Santana, Lizbeth, 61, 65–69, 119, 126, 134
De Leon, Andy, 45, 69
De León, Jason, 131–134
Dependent and Disability Pension Act (1890), 25
Deported Veterans Mural Project, 19, 64, *65*, 126, 136

Dewey Decimal Classification (DDC) system, 102–103
  306.768, *105*
  "sexual perversions," *104*
Diaz, Melanie (MelReads), 3
Dickerson, Amy, 88–89, 91–93, 127
D'Ignazio, Catherine, 17
Domby, Adam, 71
Dorchester County, Maryland. *See* Harriet Tubman Underground Railroad Byway
Douglass, Frederick, 81
Drabinski, Emily, 99–100, 107–108, 111
Du Bois, W. E. B., 85

Emancipation and the Freed in American Sculpture, 89
Equestrian Statue of Theodore Roosevelt (NYC), 19, 85–87, *87*
  contextualization, 86–87
Espinosa y Tello, Josef. *See* Plan No. 5
Estrada, Karla, 45

Faithful Slave Memorial, 84–85
  Contextualization, 85
The False Cause (Domby), 71
Figurative highlighting, 19, 78–81, 126–127
  Equestrian Statue of Theodore Roosevelt, 85–86, *87*
  The Kudzu Project, 79–80, *80*, 127
  Robert E. Lee Monument (Richmond, Virginia), *81*, *82*
Flores, Jose Avila, 45
Floyd, George, 76
Folt, Carol, 72
Fox, Violet, 103
Freeman, Theophilus, 91
Freire, Paulo, 125

Gadsden Treaty, 55
Garcia, Antero, 130

Garden Home Community Library (Oregon), 108
George, 95, *98*. See also *Melissa* (Gino)
Gino, Alex, 19, 95–98, *98*, 107–108, 119
Godoy, Monserrat, 45
Golden Gate National Recreation Area, 5
Gregory, Amos, 64, 126
Gutiérrez, Kris, 127–128
Guzman, John, 45

Harriet Tubman Underground Railroad Byway, 18, 35–36, 83, 136
historical markers, 36–38, *39*
Site 13 (*see* Harriet Tubman Underground Railroad State Park and Visitor Center)
Willow Grove Road, 36
Harriet Tubman Underground Railroad National Monument/Historical Park, 35
Harriet Tubman Underground Railroad State Park and Visitor Center, 37, *39*
birthday poster, 40, *41*
Tubman twenty, 40–42, *41*
Hartley, Roger, 84, 120
Hashtags, 78, 108, 110–111. *See also* #SharpieActivism; #somethingscoming; #UnMundoSinMuros
High Street District, 37, *39*
Hill, Jane, 96
History Lab (San Diego History Center), *138*, 139–140, *141*
Hostile Terrain 94 (HT94) *131*, 132–134, *133*
The Houma Nation, 90
How the Word is Passed (Smith), 38, 88
H.R. Bill 3786 (the relief of Harriet Tubman), 23–24
H.R. Bill 4982, 28
H.R. Report 1774, 28
Humane Borders, 132

Humanizing Deportation, 65, 68
Hunt, Christopher, 113, 115–116, *115*, 127

Indermaur, Claire McDonald, 105
The Indian, *138*, 139–140, *141*
Indigenous Sign Initiative, *11*
Ingold, Tim, 14
International Boundary Commission. *See* Boundary Commissions

Jackson, Andrew, 31–34
Jackson, H. J., 3, 9, 13
Jackson, Mahalia, *89*, 90
Janney, Caroline, 85
Jones, Martha S., 36
Jose, 45

Kaphar, Titus, 135–136
Kent, William, 7
Ketchum, David, 107
Kilgore Books (Denver, Colorado), 33–34
Kirr, Joy, 96
Klein, Dustin, 81, 83
Klein, Lauren, 17
The Kudzu Project, 79, *80*, 127
Ku Klux Klan, 73, 79, 126
Kumeyaay people, 139–140

La Casa Del Túnel, 45
The Land of Open Graves (De León), 131
Land-marking, 10–11, 59
Indigenous Sign Initiative, *11*
Muir Woods National Monument, 5–8
US–Mexico border, 55–56
Larson, Kate Clifford, x, 24, 25
Lawrence, Jacob, 37, 81
LCC. *See* Library of Congress Classification (LCC) system
Lee, Robert E., 54–55, 126
Lew, Jacob, 29, 40
Lewis, John, 81

INDEX

LGBTQIA+ literature. *See also*
  #SharpieActivism
  censorship, 116 (*see also* Book
    banning)
  characters and topics, 95–98, 112, 117
  counternarratives, 100, 127
  and transgender youth, 19, 96, 108,
    115–116
Librarians, 96, 99, 107–117
  as annotators, 99–101
Library of Congress Classification (LCC)
  system, 102, 103–106
  HQ 77.7–HQ 77.9 "Transsexualism.
    Transgenderism," *106*
  reading a call number, 106
"Like a Girl" (Lizzo), 109
Literary studies, 9
Little, Maya, 71–73, *74*, 84, 126, 136
Living a Feminist Life (Ahmed), 16
Living Literacies (Pahl & Rowsell), 12
Lizzo, 109
Long Wharf, 37
Lozano, Jairo, 45
Lucas, Henry and Maggie, *27*
Luke, Allan, 125
Lusane, Clarence, 31, 34, 135
Lyons Falls Library (New York), 108,
  109

Macedo, Donald, 125
Malone's Church, 37
Marge, 49, 88
Marginalia, 13. *See also* Literary studies
Marginalia: Readers Writing in Books
  (Jackson), 9, 17
Marginal Syllabus project, 4, 7, 10
Martin, Lawrence, 54
Mattern, Shannon, 10, 136
Matthews, Abigail, 91–92, *93*, 119, 135
Mayoral Advisory Commission on
  City Art, Monuments, and Markers,
  85–86
McCarty, Orin, 25

McClellan, Courtney, 127, 128
McKinley, William, 28
Melissa (Gino), 19, 95–118, *101*, *109*,
  110. *See also* LGBTQIA+ literature
  cataloging of, 100–107
  Library of Congress Classification, 106
  in public libraries, 107–111
  in school libraries, 112–117, *114*, *115*
Mellon, Andrew, 31, *32*, 33
Memorial landscape, 75–77, 92–93.
  See also Confederate monuments;
  Muir Woods National Monument;
  Tubman, Harriet; US–Mexico
  border
Mendez, Juana, 45
Mendoza, Tania, 45
Mesilla Treaty, 55
Methodology, 15–17
Mexican–American War, 46, 50
Miles, Tiya, 44
Minaya, Joiri, 79
Mirra, Nicole, 130
Montgomery, James, 23–24, 28
Monumental Harm (Hartley), 84
Monument critique and creativity, 19,
  71–90. *See also* Annotation as social
  activism
Monument No. 258, 18, 56, *57*, 58–59,
  58, *60*
Monument removal, New Orleans, 88
Morrissey, Katherine, 48, 58
Muir, John, 6
Muir Woods National Monument, 5
  "History Under Construction," 5, 7,
    76, 128
  Path to Preservation timeline, 5–6, *6*,
    7–8, *8*
Mules, *90*
Mural de la Hermandad (Chiu), 19,
  62–64, *63*, 126, *129*
Murillo, Alex, 45, 64–65, *65*, 68, 69,
  126
Murray, Freeman H. M., 89

National Monument Audit, 76, 94, 135
Network to Freedom Program (National
Park Service), 35
New Orleans
*Courageous, Eccentric, Diverse: New
Monuments for New Orleans*, 88–94,
89–90, *93*, 127
revision of memorial landscape, 88
Solomon Northup "12 Years a Slave"
place marker, *92*
New Revived United Methodist Church
(Taylors Island, Maryland), 37
No Common Ground, 79
North Canton Public Library (Ohio),
108
Northup, Solomon, 91, *92*, *93*

Obama, Barak, 35
O'Brien, April, 38
Olson, Hope, 102
Onondaga Free Library (New York),
111
Our Lady of Guadalupe, 45, *47*

The Padre, *138*, 139
Pahl, Kate, 12
Painter, Nell Irvin, 23, 75
Pantoja y Arriaga, Juan, 46, 51–52, 54,
125, 142
Parks, Rosa, 81
Participatory actions, 33, 40, 75, 97,
108, 116, 119–120, 132, 134–140
Pastuch, Carissa, 54
PEN America, 97
Peterson, Charles, 26
Pinchot, Gifford, 6
Plan No. 5, 51–52
Plano del Puerto de San Diego (1782),
46, 51, 125, 142
Boundary Line Linea Divisoria, 46,
52
tracing of, 46, 54 (*see also* Plan of the
Port of San Diego)

Plan of the Port of San Diego (1848), 46,
48, 51–55, *53*. *See also* San Diego–
Tijuana marge
Article V, Treaty of Guadalupe
Hidalgo, 51
Playas de Tijuana Mural Project, 19, 45,
47, 61, 65–69, *66*, *67*, 126
Polk, James, 50
Prevention Through Deterrence (PTD),
131–132
Priest, Mark, 37, *39*
Prieto, Norma Iglesias, 48, 59
Princeton Middle School (New Jersey),
113, *114*
Public memory, 38, 76, 86, 92–93
Putnam, Arthur, *138*, 139

"Queering the Catalog," (Drabinski),
99
Queer intervention
defined, 99
#SharpieActivism, 99–100, 107–108,
111
QR codes, 68, 112–113, *114*, 117

Rael, Ronald, 62, 69
Rascuache artists, 45, 137
Rasheed, Kameelah Janan, 2
Rebert, Paula, 52, 56
Reclaiming the Monument 2020, *82*
Redaction (Kaphar and Betts), 135–136
Reese, Debbie, 7, 140
Reid, Joy, 34
Re/marks
as civic compositions, 79, 91, 131–134
as critical literacy (*see* Critical literacy)
defined, 13–14
perspective on power and justice,
124
as syncretic, 127–130 (*see also*
Syncretism)
traces, 14, 56, 62, 72, 80, 99, 105, 117,
124, 134

INDEX

Report No. 787 (Committee on War
Claims), 23–24
Rivera, Isaac, 45
Robbins, Ruth Anne, 31
Robert E. Lee Monument (Richmond,
Virginia), 19, 80, *81, 82*, 83, 127
Roberto, K. R., 105
Romans 15:1, 122
Roosevelt, Theodore. *See* Equestrian
Statue of Theodore Roosevelt
Ross, Araminta. *See* Tubman, Harriet
Rowsell, Jennifer, 12
Rubsam, Robert, 2
Ruiz, Daniel, 45

Salazar, Javier, 45
San Diego History Center, 138–140, *138*
San Diego–Tijuana marge, 49
Savage, Kirk, 73
Saxon, Rufus, 23–24
Scripps, Edward W., 139
Senate Report No. 1619, 28
Shaffer, Donald, 26
Shepherd, Heyward, 84–85
Silence Sam Film, 73, *74*
Silent Sam, 19, 71–73, *74*, 85, 126
Smashing Statues (Thompson), 78–79
Smith, Clint, 38, 88, 91
Social justice, 3, 7, 10, 13–14, 38, 62, 75,
93, 124
Social media, 3. *See also* Hashtags
Bookstagram, 3
BookTok, 3
BookTube, 3
Bowties & Books, 3
Melissa (Gino), 20, 95–96, 108–112
(*see also* #SharpieActivism)
TikTok, 108–110, *109, 110*
YouTube, 3
Sorting Things Out (Bowker and Star), 102
Southern Pomo people, 6
Southern Poverty Law Center, 120
Squires, Catherine, 38

Standing Soldiers, Kneeling Slaves (Savage),
73
Stanley Institute, 37
Star, Susan, 102
Star, Wendy Red, 2
Stauffer, Andrew, 2, 16–17
Stewart, William, *27*
Stilgoe, John, 11, 49, 135
St. John, Rachel, 55
Stoughton Public Library (Wisconsin),
109–111, *110*
Syncretism, 20, 127–130, *129*, 139–140

Taylor, Breonna, 76, 81
Thompson, Erin, 78, 83–84
Trans experience, 107
Treaty of Guadalupe Hidalgo, 18, 45–46,
48, 50–51, *53*, 54–55, 125–126
Trist, Nicholas, 50–51
Trombone Shorty, 90
Trump, Donald, 78
Tubman, Harriet, 18, 23–45, 81–83, 119,
125
as annotator, 42–44, 142
Beacon of Hope (Cambridge,
Maryland), 120–123, *121*, 128
her mark, *43*
literacies of, 24–25
military service and pension, 24,
27–28
pension file, 25–26
pension file affidavits and documents,
27, 43
and Robert E. Lee Monument
(Richmond, Virginia), *82*
Special Act of Congress (1899), 28
Widow's Pension form, 28–29, *30*
Tubman Byway. *See* Harriet Tubman
Underground Railroad Byway
Tubman twenty, 18, 29–35, *34*, 40–42,
41
Tuckahoe Neck Meeting House, 37
Tung, Genevieve, 31

Twenty Dollars and Change: Harriet Tubman and the Ongoing Fight for Racial Justice and Democracy (Lusane), 31

Undocumented Migration Project, 132
University of North Carolina at Chapel Hill (UNC), 71
Upton, Aisha, 38
US–Mexico border, 18–19, 46–69
  annotations on paper (*see* Plan of the Port of San Diego)
  annotations on the wall, 46, *47*, *50*, 61–62, *63*, *65*, *67*, 68–69
  creating, via land-marking, 55–59
  first boundary survey, 56–58
  handprints, 128–129
  Monument No. 1 (original), 56, *57*, 58
  Monument No. 258 (new), 58–59, *58*, 59, *60*, 62
  second boundary survey, 59–60
  wall as annotation, 47–48, 69

Vivar, Robert, 45, 69

Wall, Dano, 33–34, 136
We Need Diverse Books, 116
Wikipedia, 4
Williams, Caroline Randall, 75

Ylarregui, José Salazar, 55